Couples

How Mindful Communication Habits Can Work Miracles in Your Relationship and Why You Need to Improve Your Communication Skills Right Now

Learn the secrets of all happy and long-lasting couples!

Levine Tatkin

accurate, up to date, and reliable, complete information. No warranties of any kind are declared or implied. Readers acknowledge that the author is not engaging in the rendering of legal, financial, medical or professional advice. The content within this book has been derived from various sources. Please consult a licensed professional before attempting any techniques outlined in this book.

By reading this document, the reader agrees that under no circumstances is the author responsible for any losses, direct or indirect, which are incurred as a result of the use of information contained within this document, including, but not limited to, — errors, omissions, or inaccuracies.

Table of Contents

Introduction

Before we begin, I would like to thank you for purchasing this book, *Couples Communication: How Mindful Communication Habits Can Work Miracles in Your Relationship and Why You Need to Improve Your Communication Skills Right Now*.

Relationships play a crucial role in how happy we are in life. A good relationship can make all the difference and help you stand firm against any adversity you might face. However, the real problem is when you have issues in your relationship itself. Everyone craves a practical and healthy relationship with a partner who loves and cherishes them as they do. However, it is not all fun and games. Relationships require effort, and a lot of people tend to forget this over time. In this book, we will discuss one of the biggest problems that most people face in their relationships—communication.

Like they say, communication is key. It is the key to a healthy relationship and genuine respect and understanding of each other. Lack of communication can cause a lot of pain and trouble to you, your partner, and others involved as well. So how well do you communicate with your partner? Do you stay calm and listen during a fight, or do you look for chances to retaliate? If you stop and think about it, you will realize how many issues could have been solved just by listening and hearing what your partner had to say instead of continually being on the defensive. Playing the blame game never helps anyone, but this is the most common approach people tend to take to avoid taking responsibility. It is important for two people to listen to each other and make an actual effort to understand what the other has to say. This is what a couple in a healthy relationship strives for.

Everyone wants a partner who listens and understands what they are trying to convey. A lack of good communication skills will affect how you express your feelings and opinions as well as how you perceive those of your partner. A partner wants to be valued and given validation in their relationship. They like sharing their interests and excitement as well as their troubles and hope to be understood by the other. But if there are communication issues and the other person is not a good listener, their partner will feel hurt and disconnected. These are the kinds of situations that can often mean the end of a relationship.

The small issues in your everyday life, as well as the big ones, can be averted or dealt with if you use mindful communication strategies like those that will be discussed in this book. Responding with respect, interest, and appreciation to your partner is something that you should constantly make an effort to do. Don't take a good relationship for granted, and take the steps necessary to make it even stronger. I hope this book helps you in this endeavor. The insights given in this book will help you build and nurture a healthy, satisfying, and cultivating a relationship with your partner.

I have seen firsthand proof of couples using these strategies and significantly improving their relationships with their partners over the years. If you are looking for a similar miracle, this is the right place for you.

Chapter 1: Mindful Communication

Communication is the key to any successful relationship. If you fail to communicate effectively, it can lead to misunderstandings, hurt feelings, and many other issues. Mindful communication is all about being more conscious about the way you interact with the other person daily. It is about being more present when the other person is communicating to you. This is especially important in a relationship. Your partner needs you to be more present, and they want to see that you can understand their thoughts and feelings. However, real communication has become increasingly difficult these days.

People are more comfortable texting each other or using social media than having actual face-to-face conversations. No matter where you look, people are looking down into their phones instead of facing the person sitting right next to them. It doesn't matter if it's on a date or if the person is sitting right next to you at home. Think about it: how often do you communicate with your partner?

Take some time and try to notice if you do any of the following things:

- Forming responses before your partner finishes their sentence
- Constantly thinking of something else even when your partner is talking to you
- Feeling impatient during a conversation
- Cutting your partner short when they speak
- Think of your own experience when they relate something that happened to them
- Feeling bored when you have to discuss something or have a real conversation

These are all some of the common communication patterns that have developed among people these days. But all of it has a negative impact on your life and your relationship with your partner. This is where mindful communication comes to the rescue. Whether you want to improve your relationship with your partner or work on your social skills in general, mindfulness adds the necessary dimension to successful communication.

Committing to mindful communication with your partner means you will be committing to the following:

- Listening to your partner without being distracted
- Holding a conversation without being too emotional
- Being non-judgmental when you talk, argue, or even fight with your partner
- Accepting your partner's perspective also if it is different from yours
- Validating yourself and your partner

All these are important and will benefit your relationship in so many ways.

Lessons from Mindful Communication

Mindful communication will help you learn some invaluable lessons. Here are a few:

You will learn to listen to your partner. Being a good listener is so important, and it is something that your partner needs from you. Don't respond without actually listening to them and letting them complete their sentences. Look them in the eye when they talk and show them that you are paying attention. Pay attention to their words and their body language. Make an effort to understand what they are trying to convey to you. Listening well can help you know your partner much better. It will also show your partner that you care. Make them more comfortable around you. They will feel valued and will know that they can depend on you.

You will learn to be non-judgemental. You will learn how to be non-judgmental and thus provide a safe space for your partner to communicate with you. People are often scared of conveying their true feelings or opinions when they think the other person will judge them. If you have a judgmental attitude, your partner will refrain from speaking honestly to you as well. This means they don't feel comfortable with you and might look for this level of understanding from someone else. Be encouraging to your partner and let them know you respect their opinion regardless of how different your own is.

You will view the problems more objectively. People often react in the wrong way when their judgment is clouded by their personal opinion or emotions. Being objective is crucial if you want to resolve issues. If not, you will not be able to have any productive or honest conversation. This is important to foster growth and solve problems in your relationship. You need to keep your partner's perspective in mind before you reply to them. The more time you take to consider their view, the better you will be able to solve a problem in an even-tempered way.

You will be able to control your life better.
Mindful communication and mindfulness, in general, can help you find more clarity in life. It will help you to avoid small problems that are often caused by bad communication. You will learn how to control your emotions and take control of how you handle various situations.

You can see that mindfulness in communication can help you truly connect with your partner. It will help you to understand them and maybe even learn from them. Your relationship will be strengthened, and you will be able to make better choices for your overall benefit. Don't doubt the value of good communication skills.

As you read the book, you will see how you can apply mindfulness in various situations and in different ways when you communicate with your partner. It will help you improve yourself as a person and increase personal growth. You will learn how to stabilize your relationship and take it in a positive direction as well. Mindful communication can teach you how to get control over your thoughts, feelings, and actions in a positive way. Once you have this control, you can exercise it for your benefit. You will soon understand how some couples make it through thick and thin just with the help of better communication.

Chapter 2: Work on Yourself First

Evaluate Yourself

Self-reflection is crucial for personal growth and plays an important role in a relationship as well. A lot of people fail to recognize their flaws and refuse to accept the mistakes made on their part. Instead, they choose to look at the other person for blame and consider themselves the victims in every situation. This can stunt a person's growth and has a very negative impact on their relationship.

Before you start working on improving your relationship with your partner, you should work on yourself. This means that you need to take a step back and look at your role in things. Think back to various situations that have taken place and look at your role in them. If you try thinking from a third person's perspective, you will see that you had an equal role in those situations as your partner. However, at that time, you might have thought otherwise. Your reaction in such circumstances will result in a lot of blame being thrown around while you speak or behave hurtfully even though you will regret it later. To avoid this, you need some time for self-reflection. Ask your partner or others for their opinion, too, if you are willing to accept it as constructive criticism.

How do you usually communicate, verbally and nonverbally (with your body language)? Many people are unaware of the fact that body language plays a bigger role in communication than words ever will. The same words said in a different tone and with different actions can have a completely different meaning. Most of the time, you can convey a lot without even saying anything to the other person. This is why it is important to work on your body language first. Improving the way you communicate with the other person will have a huge positive impact on your relationship with them. Working on yourself and identifying your shortcomings is the first part of the process if you want to improve your relationship with someone else.

It's not that you're wrong all the time or that the other person is better than you. This is not why we say that you need to work on yourself. The point is that you can always be a better version of who you are right now. There is still room for improvement, and the only one holding you back is you. If you make a little effort, you can be a better person. This will allow you to perform better in everything you do, starting from work to your relationships. To improve yourself and persist in a quest of self-improvement, there are certain steps you need to take. Self-improvement strategies will help you get started with making a positive change in your life.

For instance, break some of your usual bad habits. It could be a small habit that you considered insignificant before. You can take the initiative to change it now. If you tend to put the alarm on snooze five times before you wake up, try waking up at once from tomorrow. If you leave your bed unmade usually, make your bed as soon as you wake up. Instead of checking your social media, keep your phone away till you have had breakfast and have done some meditation. It might not be a change you want to make, but you have always known that doing these things will make your life better. So why not start doing them instead of pushing them to the back of your mind? You can easily be one of the people who are always admired if you just put in a little work on yourself. The only thing differentiating you from them is what they do that you don't. Starting with some small changes will push you to make bigger changes in the future.

Identify How You Communicate—Verbal and Nonverbal

The way you interact with others can determine a lot about how your relationships with them will pan out. How to talk to people and behave around them can say a lot about you. When you think about communication, your mind will automatically turn toward verbal communication. However, nonverbal communication plays a much larger role than you may imagine. Changing your words will not always be enough. You have to change your body language effectively too. The same words said in one tone will mean something completely different when told in a different tone. Body language is an effective way to express yourself to others, and it is time you start paying heed to it.

First, you need to understand what nonverbal communication is. Body language is not just about your posture is. There are so many other aspects involved in it. Your facial expressions and the gestures you use are all a part of your body language and convey different things to others. It has a permanent role in your life and is an important part of your social skills. You have to know how to manipulate your body language appropriately and also learn to observe that of others. When you study the body language of another person, it will help you in predicting what their reaction might be to what you say or do.

Actions can speak a lot louder than your words. There will often be times when your body language will be enough to communicate your message. When you talk, you can use your body language to reinforce the impact of your words.

When you sit with your partner, friends, or family, you need to pay attention to your body language. When they speak to you, give them your complete attention. Lean toward them and turn your body in their direction. Try to maintain eye contact. Show them that you are listening and are interested in what they have to say. Don't slouch or look away when they talk. It is disrespectful and will make them feel like you are disinterested. Your body language matters when you are arguing with someone too. Don't invade their personal space and stand or sit too close. Don't try to intimidate them with physicality. This is especially important when you are arguing with your partner. Giving off a dominating vibe will not benefit a healthy relationship. You can choose to debate over anything in a much more civil way. Avoid raising your voice and shouting at them. Don't place your hands on your hips or point your finger at them while you speak. These are all unwelcome, disrespectful displays. Don't stand over a person when they sit in front of you. Avoid intimidating gestures of this type. Exercising control and identifying this kind of body language is important.

Think of Yourself with a Critical Eye

A critical eye will help you get started with the process of changing for the better. How can you fix a problem or change something if you can't even identify or define what the problem is? One thing to take note of is that criticism should always be constructive, whether it is directed toward others or yourself. There is no point in beating yourself about something. You may make mistakes at times, and that is completely normal. It is human to make mistakes. This applies to you and others. So don't criticize in a negative non-constructive way. When someone makes a mistake or fails at something, it can be a painful experience. They don't need salt rubbed on their wound with the critical mocking words of others. However, people tend to criticize others but not themselves.

When an individual makes a mistake or faces failure, they try to take self-protective measures. They usually rationalize a situation in a way that others and they can make them look good in a positive light. Blaming others and discounting the importance of such events are common tactics. You may feel better after doing this, but it will not help you grow as a person. This kind of behavior will not help you avoid mistakes in the future either. Instead of focusing your critical eye on others, why not try some self-criticism for a change? No matter how good you may think you are, there is always room for improvement, and it is important to accept this. Having an over-inflated perception of yourself will prevent you from working toward personal growth with time.

Self-criticism is easier said than done. Very few people dare to face their inner demons. When you take an honest look at yourself, you might feel quite despaired and hopeless. This, in turn, may cause you to blame yourself and beat yourself up for all that you are lacking. This kind of self-criticism will not benefit you in any way. You will just be making things harder for yourself. Being hard on yourself will not make you a better person. Research shows that it can make you procrastinate more and be even slower in working toward your goals. This kind of criticism will make you feel incompetent and might prevent you from making the little effort you previously made to.

The following tips will help you constructively conduct self-criticism.

Be specific about what you criticize. Choose to criticize aspects of yourself that you have control over and can change. Don't focus on unchangeable attributes and waste your energy. If you sit and think that you are not intelligent, it will just make you depressed and affect your self-esteem. This kind of thinking does not help, and it is unnecessary. Instead, be more optimistic and explanatory while focusing on something specific. Tell yourself that you could have done much better on your tests if you did not waste so much time watching TV. This kind of critical reasoning will help you identify what the problem is and give you a solution as well.

Identify the situation that is the cause of the problem. Sometimes, all the blame cannot be placed on you. There might be circumstances or a situation that pushed you to take the wrong steps. For instance, you might have failed your test because you were up all night and did not study well. However, this could be because your roommate had friends over and there was too much noise. I'm not saying that you can use this as an excuse. Instead, this kind of situation gives you leverage. When you know you cannot study in this kind of situation, you have to find an alternate solution. Go to the library or study at a friend's place. You have to take responsibility for the result, but you also need to take the situation into account. Everyone is vulnerable to some external pressures, so it is important to be aware of them and prevent being blindsided.

Stop focusing only on yourself and think of others too. Think of how your actions may affect others. Don't be too caught up in self-criticism. Broaden your focus and think of the relationships you want to nurture. Your goals need to be more compassionate and less about self-image. These kinds of goals will help in preventing conflicts in your relationship and receiving support. Don't be so focused on protecting your ego and self-esteem that you view everyone as a threat or competition. It is important to recognize what your partner and other people need too.

Practice self-compassion when you criticize yourself. Self-criticism becomes more bearable when you pair it with self-compassion. Don't let shame overpower your emotions and prevent you from using the criticism for your benefit. There might be parts of you that you are afraid of looking at. But if you practice self-compassion, it will be like a cushion to fall back on even when you receive a blow. You will be able to accept your flaws and failures even while remaining kind to yourself. Yes, you made a mistake, but that mistake does not define you as a bad person. Every person has his or her strengths and weaknesses. It is important to recognize both and try to turn the weaknesses into strengths.

Self-Validation

Self-validation means you start accepting your internal experience and learn to build a positive identity.

Validation is how you show a person that you understand and accept their thoughts, feelings, actions, etc. Validation itself plays a crucial role in your relationship with your partner. We will delve more into this in another section of the book. Here you will learn more about the importance of self-validation. The same way that you accept and acknowledge others, you need to be more accepting and understanding of yourself. Your thoughts and your emotions are all valid. However, you should not assume that they are always correct or justified. Self-validation is not the same as self-justification. Your thoughts may often go against the grain and surprise you. You may sometimes do things that are not reflective of your core values. You might have feelings or thoughts that make you uncomfortable. You need to stop fighting these off and refrain from judging yourself or anyone else for having these thoughts and feelings.

Learning to observe and acknowledge your thoughts and feelings will help you learn and grow as a person. Giving validation to your opinions and emotions will help you remain calm and have better control over yourself. When you self-validate, you learn to understand and accept yourself better. It will allow you to build a stronger identity and be better skilled at managing wayward emotions that might otherwise drive you in the wrong direction.

Notice how we use *"mindful" communication* in the title of the book. Even when you are working on yourself, mindfulness will go hand in hand with self-validation. You need to be mindful of what you think or feel for you to validate them.

Levels of Self-Validation

Self-validation happens at six different levels.

1. To be aware of your feelings without pushing them away goes hand in hand with being more present. Being present means that you have to ground yourself and not separate, daydream, stifle, or numb your feelings. You have to learn to listen to yourself. It can be unpleasant to experience sadness or fear. However, if you keep avoiding your feelings, they can build up and result in very negative outcomes. On the other hand, accepting enables feelings to pass and helps you to become more resilient to all the challenges you face. Being present will help in self-validation and the realization that you matter and that you are allowed to feel. Your emotional experience is just as valid as any other experience in your life.

2. Reflection means to manifest or to make something evident. Self-validation requires accurate reflection; it is recognizing your inner state to yourself and being able to label it accurately. Maybe you think about what set off the feeling and when it occurred. Perhaps you might ponder over how you feel that emotion in your body and consider the actions that go with that feeling. Reflecting methods involve watching and depicting as aspects of mindfulness. When you reflect over your inward experience, you don't translate or theorize or make presumptions. You can state, "I feel furious, and it began yesterday after my companion canceled plans with me. I can feel a gripping sensation in my stomach, and perhaps there is a feeling of dread." Saying, "I am an absolute failure, and nobody needs to invest their time on me," would not be expressing the certainties of your experience. Conveying a certain fact from your experience involves validation and enables you to trust your

personal experience. If you interpret your experiences in a bogus manner, you negate and prompt doubt as far as you can tell.

3. You will not always be sure of what you feel or think. This is when you might say things like, "This kind of situation usually makes other people sad, but I don't know if I am sad." Guessing can be done by thinking of the actions that you want to take. If you feel like hiding from someone, you probably feel shameful about facing them. Maybe you did something that makes you ashamed, and your body will give you sensations like tightness in your throat in such cases. You can guess how you are feeling or thinking if you evaluate the information about the situation that you already have.

4. Events from your past can also dictate your thoughts or feelings at times. You may be uncomfortable when people argue in front of you. This can be because you got hurt in this kind of a situation in the past. This often

happens when people undergo some abusive or traumatic experience. That same kind of situation can trigger feelings of fear or upset even in the present, and this is understandable. You have to validate based on history as well.

5. Intense emotions can sometimes be hard to process and accept. When you experience some intense emotion, you might feel like you are abnormal for being this way. You think it is not a normal way of thinking or feeling. However, emotions are a part of human life. Everyone experiences emotions, and the intensity of emotions varies for everyone. You are allowed to be as hurt, angry, sad, or ashamed as you feel. You have to validate your feelings and also validate when someone else feels this way. The situation you are going through would probably incite the same kind of feelings or thoughts in other people. You can find out or ask others if they would feel the same way in such situations. It will help you normalize and validate your own experiences.

6. You can be genuine and stop lying to yourself. Be your real self. Don't pretend to be what you are not. If you reject your truth, it is one of the worst ways to deny yourself validation. You have to understand that what you do is not always equal to who you are. You are not defined by your behavior. If you feel uncomfortable or recognize bad behavior, changing it a little will help you accept yourself much easier.

Learn how to self-validate because it is a critical step in living a better life. It will help you form healthy relationships with others and thrive on them. You have to instill self-validation in your everyday practices until it becomes a way of being for you.

Chapter 3: The Impact of Ego on Your Life and Relationship

Egoism

"Ego"—this word will always have more negativity associated with it than positivity. Everyone has an ego, whether they wish to acknowledge it or not. The important thing is to learn to control your ego. When your ego overpowers the love you have for your partner, it can mean the end of your relationship or at least cause many issues in it. This section of the book is focused on identifying the impact of ego in a relationship and learning how to deal with it. If you or your partner has a big ego, it will give rise to a lot of problems that could otherwise be resolved quite easily. You have to learn how to control your ego and also how to deal with a partner who might have a big ego. Ego can give rise to a lot of negative feelings, like fear, anger, resentment, and jealousy. None of these will do anything beneficial for you or your relationship. So if you want to learn how to deal with egoism properly, read on.

People are often confused when they talk about ego. Ego is present in every person, but there is a healthy and unhealthy amount of ego that makes a difference. A healthy ego is not the same as a huge ego. If you have a strong ego, you have to be willing to deflate your ego for the benefit of your relationship. A huge ego may drive you to sabotage your relationship, and this is when the troubles arise.

Love will always draw you toward what is good. It moves us to be caring and sensitive with our partner, and it reproves us when we are cruel or careless. It is not about habits or your upbringing; the power of affection in us is what makes us feel so uneasy with being irate, discourteous, responsive, nervous, or jumpy toward our partner. If you follow your heart, your ego will not get a chance to play much of a negative role in your relationship. Love should always govern your thoughts and actions.

However, your ego can be a powerful force. If your

love is egotistical, you will make decisions based on your ego instead of following your heart. Your heart and love will guide you to do what is right for your relationship. Your ego will only let you make decisions that are selfish and in your favor, not for the benefit of your relationship or your partner. The choices you make with your ego will be an obstacle for a happy relationship. With an end goal to reassure ourselves, the ego will retreat to opposition, contention, battle, mockery, put-downs, gloom, withdrawal, hostility, dissatisfaction, passive-aggressive behavior, vengeance, disrespect, narrow-mindedness, fault, rivalry, doubt, disdain, and self-doubt, etc. Your ego is not wired to solve problems rationally and think in the best interest of your relationship. If your ego is too big, you will always be focused on protecting yourself from the hurt that love can cause you. Your sense of self-protection will be too great to allow you to shed your barriers in front of your partner. Instead, you will constantly make an effort to keep the walls up and prevent any harm to yourself.

Egoistic love is an impression of the necessities, needs, and wants of the one, not the other. It is based upon the mistaken reasoning that our sense of fulfillment can be found in another. We place our interest in that other person so that they are every one of the things that we need her or him to be. It demands that they be something that they can't in any way, shape, or form be—that is, the thing that we need that person to be instead of what or who that person is. This can prompt thwarted expectations, disillusionment, and at last, resentment. These things will eventually break a relationship.

Signs That Ego Is Ruining Your Relationship

Blaming

If you are always reprimanding or blaming your partner for everything, you need a rude awakening. This happens when your ego is controlling your relationship and utilizing manipulative tactics to do it. Do you ever assume responsibility for the things that you do? Would you be able to move to one side and think from another perspective without accusing the other person? The ego will want you to find fault and scrutinize for others' mistakes. It will do everything and anything to transfer blame and criticize another person. Shockingly, that thing we evade is generally what we end up receiving in our relationships. If you fail to take responsibility for yourself, your ego will help you project all this onto your partner.

Playing the Victim

Is it safe to say that you are playing the unfortunate victim card in your relationship? Do you always compare yourself with your partner? Is it true that you are continually putting yourself down? An unhealthy ego will help you reinforce negative actions as opposed to positive ones. It will cause you to focus too much on your imperfections. If you are doing this, it is unquestionably time to venture back and conduct a recheck on your relationship. You are not a saint. The time has come to be responsible for what you are bringing to the table and stop constantly blaming your partner for everything.

Being Jealous

Jealousy is the green-eyed monster, and it usually sets the stage for negative drama in a relationship. Ego tends to feed on self-esteem and the absence of acknowledgment. A cherishing relationship depends on regard and consciousness of each other. Love doesn't contribute to comparing, putting down, and criticizing as ego does. This is a show that turns into the most astounding type of negative drama in any relationship. If you are in an abusive relationship, your ego won't let you leave because of jealousy. What is making you consider these ideas? Does your partner make you question the validity of your relationship? This means you need to venture back and be straightforward about identifying the abuse in the relationship.

Fearing Rejection

This kind of dread prevents you from proceeding onward and accomplishing any of your goals. When you stop yourself as a result of this dread, you are unfair to your relationship. Changing the way you perceive things as opposed to being incapacitated by the anxiety and uneasiness caused by your ego will be a healthy way to increase self-esteem. Negative self-talk will only feed your ego. Don't compromise on who you truly are to surrender to your partner's ego. This is anything but healthy. A loving relationship depends on mutual respect and acknowledgment. On the off chance that you are feeling rejected, maybe it's time to re-evaluate your relationship.

Always Having the Last Word

Your ego has a way of making every little thing about you and turning it into a one-person play. If you find that you talk a lot about yourself and don't ask about your partner, well, you are immensely ego-driven.

The ego assumes a superb role in shielding us from accomplishing total harmony and joy. It is the mind's method for controlling. It will likewise create situations in your mind that don't exist. If you find that you need to have the last say in all things, it's time that you venture back and discover the root of this need. Do you feel like you are better than others or second rate? Do you lack self-confidence and, in this manner, need to demonstrate that you are worthy despite all the trouble? The ego will make you conceal your sense of mediocrity by overhyping yourself. If you and your partner fight a lot, your ego probably fuels these fights. Is this how you feel important in your relationship?

It is important to take a step back and observe your relationship at times. You need to identify when you are the one in the wrong and making mistakes. Take a look at your actions and acknowledge when they are driven by ego. You have to let go of your ego if you want a strong, healthy relationship with your partner.

So if you have a big ego or your love is egotistical, what should you do?

For the narcissist, being correct all the time is deeply connected with their sense of self-worth. In this way, the individuals who can't relinquish their ego do and say anything they want, and they always think they are correct. Tragically, this will be at the expense of a lot of other things. Their need to always be correct can cost them their relationship with colleagues, supervisors, kin, relatives, and more often than not, their partners. Sooner or later, you have to understand that the bogus self-esteem that you get from adhering to your ego and "being correct" doesn't exceed genuine happiness.

Being true to yourself and practicing mindfulness will enable you to understand that you can't be right in every circumstance. There will be certain situations where you make a mistake, you have a wrong mentality, or you're essentially on the wrong side. Figure out how to discern these kinds of circumstances, and don't be hesitant to concede that you are in the wrong.

It may be hard to admit this at times; however, having the ability to concede when you're wrong can be quite liberating. Assume responsibility for your actions and decisions, and you will soon see that the ball will be in your court!

You don't have to be better or greater than everyone around you. The need to be this way can be quite destructive for you. A great sense of ego leads you to believe that you are superior to every other person. It is similar to remembering that you don't need to be correct constantly. Understand that you don't have to be better than everybody else either. That is not a healthy level of competitiveness in anyone.

There will always be somebody better, prettier, more astute, quicker, wealthier than you. No matter how old you are, this will always be the way of things. The sooner you understand that you cannot — and ought not to feel committed to — be superior to other people, the sooner you can repair and improve your relationships.

Rather than contending with others along these lines, why not consider improving yourself? You are perfectly unique. Focus on how you can improve yourself, and every one of your relationships will take a turn for the better.

Dealing with a Person with a Huge Ego

We have talked enough about ego in general and how to control your ego. Now let's discuss more how to deal with a partner with a big ego. More often than not, the male in the relationship tends to have ego issues. This is a common issue in many relationships that women have to contend with. A lot of the time, this ego issue can give rise to serious problems in a relationship. If your partner has a really big ego, he will be more inclined to demonstrate anger, frustration, and irritation at the smallest provocation. You need to know when your partner has a healthy amount of self-confidence and when it borders on unhealthy ego.

Here are the signs that your partner has too much ego:

1. ***They need to be the center of attention.*** You will notice that they constantly want people to focus on them, and they feel uncomfortable when the attention is turned toward someone else. They might have seemed like a fun, outgoing person at first, but when you pay attention, you will see that it is all an effort to attract attention solely toward them.

2. ***They always make things about them.*** Even when you are sad or celebrating something, it ultimately becomes about them. Instead of consoling you when you are sad, they will start relating their own sad story. You will be the one consoling most of the time instead of receiving support. When you want to celebrate an achievement, they will talk about all their achievements.

3. ***They always shift the blame on you instead of acknowledging their mistake.*** They will run away from confrontation when they are the one at fault. You will end up apologizing or forgiving without ever receiving an apology from them. They will try to make you feel guilty even when they are the ones who should be feeling that way.

4. ***They tend to talk about themselves a lot.*** They will somehow turn the topic around and make it about them. You have to notice if your partner makes an effort to listen to you. If they have a big ego, they will be the one who talks more in the relationship. If you ask them about something you told them, they will usually fail to remember because they never paid attention. They will hijack any conversation and are only interested in making it all about them.

5. ***They will hate taking advice from you.*** It hurts their ego to acknowledge that you might know better than them at times. They won't acknowledge it even if what you said turns out to be right. They will want the credit for themselves. They will hate accepting that they might not know something or that they made a mistake.

6. ***They will always compare themselves to others and try to show that they are better.*** They will find ways to show you that they are somehow better than you and others around you. They will even choose to criticize your friends or family and prove to you that they are inferior to him.

7. ***They will be very critical of everything about you.*** They will criticize the way you dress, talk, do things, etc. They want to create a

sense of doubt in you and boost their ego instead. Their criticism will never be constructive but instead will just hurt you.

If you notice these signs in your partner, he or she is a self-serving egoistic person. You can choose to walk away from this kind of person. However, you might want to work on it and try to improve things as well. Don't be submissive to another person's unhealthy ego and sacrifice your own. Find a way to make them change and acknowledge their mistakes. You both need to find a healthy balance in your relationship so that their ego does not compromise your happiness.

Start communicating your opinions and feelings. Don't hold back and feed their ego. You don't have to fight or shout. You can do it calmly and let them know how you feel or think about things. If you were previously submissive, they might be surprised at the change in you; thus, you need to wait for them to get used to it. Be wary of someone who gets aggressive when you do so.

Start saying no when you need to. You don't have to agree to everything they say. They might want to control what you do or where you go. You don't have to accommodate unreasonable demands made by them. Be clear and tell them that your personal needs and desires are just as important as theirs. If they have the freedom to do as they please, so do you.

Give advice but don't force it on them. It is up to any individual to heed another person's advice. But when what you say proves to be true or helpful, make them acknowledge it. You can calmly remind them that you had been the one who had said so and that they might benefit from listening to you in the future at times.

Don't force an egoist to apologize. They will resent you for it and turn the tables on you. Let them know that you think they are in the wrong but don't force them to apologize. They have to learn to do this themselves, and it might take some time.

Don't ask for permission to do things from an egoist. It will feed their ego and an unhealthy need to control your life. Let them know that you are responsible for yourself and not a child who needs their consent to do things.

Encourage a healthy change in behavior in that person. When they do something good and different from their usual tendencies, encourage them. Remember to control this and not flatter them too much. Just let them know what you appreciate and acknowledge and what you don't. Don't feed their ego with excessive praise. Just articulate your appreciation for good behavior in the right way, but do it moderately.

Reassure them about their insecurities to make them get over it healthily. It is important to be supportive of your partner. Their insecurities can often make them behave irrationally to conceal it. Don't poke at their insecurities. Reach out and comfort them instead of birthing them out of resentment.

Make them realize they need you and that they need to appreciate what you do for them. Don't let them take you for granted. Make them see that their egoistic actions might make them lose you.

Keeping these pointers in mind will help you deal with a partner who has a weak ego. You should also know how to control your ego to prevent jeopardizing your relationship. I hope this section helped you gain a better understanding of the topic of egos in relationships.

Chapter4: Misunderstandings— How to Prevent or Resolve Them

Misunderstandings are often one of the main reasons that relationships face disruption. It could be any relationship—one with your partner, with your friends, colleagues, or even your family. But if you make an effort, you can generally avoid such misunderstandings or at least resolve them amicably. When your relationship is free of misunderstandings, you will experience peace of mind and be much happier with your partner. This is why I have dedicated a section of this book to deal with the topic of misunderstandings.

There are very few people who can say that they have never had a misunderstanding in their entire life. Misunderstandings are quite common, and nearly everyone is disturbed by one at some point or the other. A misunderstanding can make you feel confused and distraught. It can affect your balanced state of mind and affect your relationship with the person involved in this misunderstanding.. If this person is your partner, the misunderstanding can be especially harmful. No matter how reliable and sturdy your relationship usually is, a misunderstanding can throw it off balance. There are so many unfortunate people who have broken off relationships with their significant others based on a single misunderstanding. Can you now get an idea of just how significant misunderstandings can be and why you need to avoid them?

So what is a misunderstanding? If you look at the word itself, you will see that it is the failure to understand or comprehend something properly. A misunderstanding has nothing right in it. It means you have failed to correctly understand a situation, a person, or the meaning behind their actions. A quarrel or disagreement is also a misunderstanding at times. It is a misinterpretation or distortion of what the reality is. This is why misunderstandings leave the wrong impression on a person's mind. When you understand someone's words or actions in the wrong way, it is a misunderstanding. You may not realize it, but you have probably misunderstood your partner on many occasions as well. They might have done the same as well. The drawback is that it can be a real cause for trouble in your relationship and is probably one of the main reasons you both end up quarreling or upset with each other.

A misunderstanding does not always arise directly from how you communicate with a person. It can even be caused by a lack of communication. What you say, how you act, the way you move, or even all that you don't do can give rise to misunderstandings in your relationship. For instance, when you don't call your partner for an entire day, they might misunderstand and assume you do not care for them. The real reason might be that you lost your phone, fell sick, or were just too busy. These petty misunderstandings can cause unnecessary trouble in paradise. But in general, a misunderstanding is usually miscommunication and not the same as lack of communication. Misunderstandings can be one-sided or even on the part of both partners. You might both misunderstand the other and interpret a situation, which in reality does not warrant any ill feelings.

What Causes Misunderstandings?

Various reasons can cause misunderstandings between you and your partner. Below are some of the common causes:

- Words are interpreted in the wrong way and different from what the other person was trying to convey.
- Something is not conveyed or explained in the right way, and the other person fails to understand.
- You have prejudice and set notions in your mind that prevent you from making an unbiased interpretation.
- Past behavior or instances are used as a reference, and your opinion is made based on them instead of the present.

- A third person influences your thoughts and opinions. They can make you see things from their perception, and you may fail to see things with clarity.
- You incorrectly assess a situation or a person.
- You fail to understand the context of the matter.
- You already mistrust the other person.
- There are feelings of envy or jealousy.
- There is a lack of self-esteem or self-confidence.
- You get carried away by emotions.

There are plenty of other reasons that can make you or your partner misunderstand each other. But more often than not, they occur when either of you assumes things or gets too emotional and fails to look at the situation with clarity. In such cases, the assumptions you make will rarely have any justifiable reason and will be a projection of your emotions or thoughts.

Misunderstandings can happen in so many different ways. These days, there are more misunderstandings because of the prominent virtual world. There is so much miscommunication as well as misinterpretation of reality because of texts, images, etc. What you see will often make you assume things quite instantly. When you read something, you might be thinking of a different tone than what the person intended to write with. Presumptions are usually made by the person who views or receives these kinds of messages and texts when the sender is unable to express clearly. Such presumptions lead to misunderstandings. This is why we emphasize the importance of face-to-face conversations.

How to Prevent Misunderstandings?

It's been known for quite some time that great relationships are based on great communication. Communication is significant since it is only through conversations and opening up to each other that two individuals can truly expand on the bond that they have with each other. However, regularly, we find that the end of a generally strong and cheerful relationship is miscommunication and misconception. One thing can be said and can be seen in a very surprisingly different way from how it was intended, and this can usually prompt pointless fights that can annihilate any feelings of closeness and fondness in a relationship.

This is why you should make it a point to practice mindful communication with your partner regularly. Both of you should make an effort to have meaningful conversations that will help you to be transparent with each other. You should make it a point to always share whatever is at the forefront of your thoughts or in your heart. In the meantime, you need to give your partner the sort of room and opportunity that they need to communicate well with you too. You should try your best to always listen well to your partner. You need to focus, and you need to truly listen to what they're trying to let you know. Keep in mind that communication is not just about saying whatever it is you need to say. It's about the steady trade of thoughts and emotions between two partners in a relationship. It's tied with taking note of your partner's thoughts and feelings and attempting to see things from their point of view.

In the end, we are all just human, and we are always prone to mistakes from time to time. That is all right. It's ordinary. Yet in those instances of shortcoming, it's important for us to try our best and take the appropriate actions to rectify our mistakes.

If you and your partner have been battling with misunderstandings in your relationship, you may find it confusing and troubling concerning how to approach settling them. Maybe you incidentally hurt your partner because of a misconception, or your partner hurt you and you're trying to manage the issue. By figuring out how to speak with the one you cherish and becoming more attuned to the importance behind each other's words, you can appreciate all the more satisfying relationship.

Paying attention and listening to your partner is vital to clearing up any misconceptions that are controlling your relationship in a negative way. Rather than simply waiting for one person to quit talking to say your bit, make it a point to concentrate on what he or she is saying. Listening is an important ability in creating and keeping up a healthy relationship. You ought to listen in order to see, as opposed to concentrating on how you need to react to argue what your partner is saying.

Establish common expectations in your relationship to clear up and stay away from problems later on. For instance, you may agree on the sort of atmosphere you appreciate at home or the limits with regard to past relationships. Moreover, realizing how to best approach your partner when it comes to sensitive issues is useful to counteract misconceptions. You will learn that most couples don't have a habit of verbalizing what they need and want, and this is a drawback.

While emails and messages are common methods for communication, they can prompt a lot of misunderstandings in a relationship. It's difficult to sympathize with your partner when you can't even see their face or look into their eyes. On the off chance that your partner misjudges what you truly implied in an email or instant message, make sure to account for yourself and clarify that you didn't finish the message you were trying to convey since it was only a short text. If these types of issues come up regularly, you both should decide to stop using electronic mediums for communicating. In case this isn't a choice, make a point to keep your electronic communication brief, and don't raise any significant life issues in an instant message. You should not be fighting or breaking up over texts or social media.

If it so happens that your partner does something that confuses you or says something hurtful to you, don't make a hasty judgment about what their conduct or words mean. Maybe they were attempting to state something different but failed to convey it appropriately. Be purposeful about assuming the best about your partner. Rather than responding with resentment on account of something she stated, take a few steps back and ask them what they implied by that specific statement. By not making a hasty judgment, you will clear up misconceptions in your relationship, just as you figure out how to see each other in a more positive light.

Resolving Misunderstandings

Keep the following pointers in mind the next time any misunderstandings arise in your relationship. It is important to address them and resolve them as soon as possible to avoid any lasting negativity.

Keep in mind not to sweat the little stuff. Rather than making every little issue a mountain, consent to not make something a fight unless it's really of significance. Understand that few out of every odd argument should be an actual fight. This doesn't mean you bow to another person's requests when it's something you feel firmly about. Make an effort to scrutinize the dimension of the significance of the current issue.

Practice acknowledgment. Any time that you wind up in a fight, attempt to recall that the other individual is coming into this situation with an entirely different mindset and set of experiences than yourself. You have not been in your partner's shoes, and you should keep in mind that it might help to place yourself in them. Your partner is the only one who can truly clarify where they are coming from and what they are feeling or thinking.

Exercise patience. Truly, it's difficult to recall this without giving it much thought. Be that as it may, stopping to take a few breaths and choosing to enjoy a reprieve and return to the problem when tempers are not as high can, most of the time, be the ideal approach to manage the current circumstance.

Lower your expectations. This isn't to say you ought to have low expectations. However, it is to state that you should remember you both might have different expectations. The ideal approach to illuminate this is to ask what your partner expects in a situation. Once more, don't consequently accept that you come into the circumstance with similar expectations.

Be that as it may, imagine a scenario in which you are in a heated argument, and you both now decide to do something other than criticize each other.

Keep in mind you both want congruity. No doubt, you both need to refocus if you want a peaceful relationship. Take time to recollect the deep connection that you both had. It's difficult to feel angered and misunderstood by somebody when you consider yourselves to be interconnected and moving in the direction of a similar outcome.

Concentrate on the conduct of the individual and not their attributes. Harsh words can unquestionably be very harming and long-lasting. Discuss what behavior upsets you rather than what is "wrong" with their identity.

Ask them what was implied by their actions or words rather than what you saw their activity to mean. More often than not, your partner isn't intentionally attempting to harm you, and you getting hurt happened to be a side effect of what they did.

Remember that your goal is to take care of the issue, not to win the fight. Fight the temptation to prove you are right all the time. Keep in mind that it's smarter to resolve the issue and find common ground.

Acknowledge your partner's reaction. When you have shared your sentiments concerning the impact of their actions or words on you, acknowledge their reaction. If they tell you that they did not intend to hurt you, take them at their word. Trust in your partner.

Let it go once you have resolved the issue. When you've both had the chance to share your side, commonly consent to let it go. Ideally, your exchange will end in a commonly acceptable manner. If it doesn't, you may return to it later. When settling on this choice, ask yourself if it is an important issue for you. When you decide to settle on the decision to let it go, do your best to do that, as opposed to bringing it up again in future arguments.

Misunderstandings can be troubling. However, if you consider it to be an open door for development, it can enable you to get closer and improve your relationship.

Chapter 5: The Power of Validation

When we consider what we can do to sustain our relationship, we tend to think of tangible ways: Get her precious jewelry, Take her out for a fancy dinner. Surprise your spouse with fancy lingerie. Buy them flowers and chocolate. Take a romantic trip together.

While these things unquestionably won't hurt your relationship (by any stretch of the imagination!), they aren't the most grounded approaches to connect with your partner. A happy couple does not survive for long based purely on these things.

The more profound part of your relationship has more to do with how you connect instead of what you do together. It is called validation. Acknowledgment of your partner's thoughts and sentiments is the best thing you can accomplish for your relationship.

Recollect back to the time when you last felt truly understood. Maybe it was a good teacher in school who appeared to know precisely the best thing to say when you were disturbed. Perhaps it was your partner who dropped everything when you called with some exciting news and were anxious to share your happiness. Recollect the last time you truly felt heard, comprehended, and tuned in to. It's a groundbreaking feeling. That is the power of validation.

Validation in your relationship is a similar thought. It implies that when your partner talks to you about their day or shares their emotions, you choose to remain present with them at the time, respecting their experience. You join their reality and see things from their perspective. It's a method for demonstrating that you comprehend and acknowledge their thoughts and sentiments, as they seem to. Research has shown that having these sorts of conversations with your partner helps your partner feel more confident and strong. Negating practices, on the other hand, do the inverse; they make your partner feel reprimanded, ignored, or hated by you.

Relationships that are the best are those where the two partners share their inner thoughts (their genuine feelings, emotions, and wants) and where their partner, in turn, can truly hear them. When you share a validating style of communication, you construct trust and closeness. These are the bonds that make relationships last.

While the idea of validation may appear to be straightforward, it can now and again be somewhat difficult to execute.

Envision that your partner gets back home and reveals to you that they are angry because they discovered they have to work even on holiday. What is your first response? A large number of us would feel defensive of our companion or agitated with the circumstance and have the natural desire to try to help or fix the situation. You may offer some advice on the most proficient method to tackle this problem. While it naturally feels accommodating to give such advice, this can feel negating to your partner. Your partner may not be searching for assistance with resolving the issue; they most likely have already tried to discover approaches to take care of the issue and may feel more irritated in hearing what you say regardless of how good your intentions were.

Invalidation

Invalidation is the point at which an individual's opinions and sentiments are dismissed, overlooked, or judged. Negation is sincerely annoying for anybody yet especially frightful for somebody who is genuinely quite sensitive.

Invalidation disturbs connections between couples and causes separation. At the point where two people invalidate each other, they create distance and make it hard to tolerate their partner.

Self-negation and refutation by another person can make recovering from disheartenment and uneasiness, especially troublesome. A lot of people believe that invalidation can escalate troublesome issues in a relationship.

A great many people would deny that they negate their partner's experiences. Not very many would intentionally refute another person. In any case, some individuals might be awkward with dealing with strong feelings and trust that they are helping when they are nullifying.

Regarding self-invalidation, numerous individuals would agree that they nullify themselves yet would contend that they deserve it. They may state that they don't deserve that sort of validation. They are not comfortable with their very own humanness. Validation isn't self-acknowledgment; it is just an affirmation that an inner experience even happened.

Verbal Invalidation

There is a wide range of reasons and ways that individuals who care about you invalidate you. Here are a few of these reasons:

Misconstruing What It Means to Be Close

Sometimes, individuals believe they know exactly how another person feels without asking. It implies they are sincerely close to their partner. It is the same as saying they understand you just as you most likely are, so they don't ask. They accept and may even reveal to you how you think and feel.

The Misconception of What It Means to Validate

Sometimes, your partner may invalidate your feelings or thoughts because validation will mean that they agree to you. An individual can state, "You believe it's wrong that you're irate with your companion," and still not be agreeing with you. Validation is not the same as agreeing. But since they need to console you, they might invalidate by saying, "You shouldn't be feeling that way."

Needing to Fix Your Feelings

"Please, don't be upset. Need some chocolate?" People who adore you don't want to see you hurting, so sometimes they discredit your thoughts and sentiments in their attempt to get you to feel a little better.

Not Wanting to Hurt Your Feelings

Sometimes, your partner may lie to you to not offend you. Perhaps they might say to you that you look incredible in a dress that in truth isn't the best style for you. Perhaps they agree with your perspective in an argument when, in reality, they don't think you are sensible.

They Want the Best for You

People who cherish you will usually want the best for you. So they may want to do things for you that you could easily do yourself. Or on the other hand, they urge you to make friends with somebody who has an influential position even when you don't generally like that individual. They might tell you that that individual is an extraordinary friend even when it's not valid. "You ought to be more friendly with her. She'll be a decent companion to you."

There is likewise a wide range of methods for invalidation. I've recorded a couple them down in the next section beneath.

Accusing

"You are always such a crybaby, vexed about something or the other, and ruining every occasion." "Why didn't you fill gas in the vehicle before you came home? You never think, and always make everything more difficult." Blaming is continually invalidating your partner. (Accusing is not the same as assuming responsibility.)

Hoovering

Hoovering is the point at which you attempt to vacuum up any sentiments you are awkward with or not give honest answers since you would prefer not to be upset or to be helpless. Saying, "It's not a big deal," when it is important to you is hoovering. Saying somebody worked well when they didn't or that your other friends loved meeting them when they didn't is hoovering. Not recognizing how troublesome something may be for you to do is hoovering. Saying, "No issue I can do that," even when you feel overwhelmed, is hovering.

Judging

"You are so going overboard" and "That is a ludicrous idea" are instances of judging and invalidating. Mocking is an especially harming habit: "Here we go once more. Cry over nothing. Let those huge tears stream down."

Denying

"You are not furious. I know how you act when you are really angry." "You are so much. I know you're not hungry anymore." These lines invalidate the other individual by saying they don't feel what they are saying that they feel.

Limiting

"Don't stress. It's nothing, and you're simply going to keep yourself sleepless over nothing" is normally said with the best of goals. Still, the message is not to feel what you are feeling.

Nonverbal Invalidation

Nonverbal nullification is quite powerful and incorporates eye-rolls and drumming of fingers anxiously. On the off chance that somebody checks their watch while you are chatting with them, it can be invalidating. Appearing at a significant occasion but choosing to focus on checking emails or playing games on the phone while you are there is also invalidating. This is regardless of whether that is the message the individual intended to send or not.

Nonverbal self-invalidation is done by working excessively, shopping excessively, or generally not focusing on your sentiments, wants, or needs.

Replace Invalidation with Validation

The ideal approach to quit invalidating others, your partner, or yourself is by rehearsing validation. Validation is never about lying—or then again, about agreeing. It's tied in with tolerating another person's inner experience as legitimate and reasonable. It can be exceptionally powerful for your relationship.

How do you show validation to your partner?

Ask yourself some questions to see if you have been giving validation to your partner.

- Do you let them know that their words matter to you?
- Do you express compassion to them when they show they are hurt?
- Have you let them know that their words have left an impression on you?
- Have you told them that you want to understand them on an emotional level?

- Do you tell them that you accept and acknowledge their feelings even when they might differ from your own?

Think of all this, and if the answer is in the negative, you have failed to provide validation to your partner on most occasions.

So how would you successfully listen to and validate your partner? There are a couple of key parts to help control your discussions.

Careful listening is the main part of validation. This implies you truly focus on what your partner is saying. As troublesome as it may be, suspend your responses to the circumstance or a topic. Briefly let go of the need to exhort, change, help, or fix the circumstance. Your considerations should be set aside for later; your center, rather, is on your partner's present experience. Show them that you are tuning in by ceasing what you are doing (shutting the workstation, turning off the TV), turning your body toward them, gesturing your head, and looking at them as they talk.

Acknowledging and being tolerant is the subsequent stage invalidation. This implies you recognize what they've been saying or what they are feeling. You may state, "I can see you're disturbed about this," or "You appear to be very discouraged," in light of their news about working throughout the end of the week. As opposed to attempting to perk your partner up, you give them space to be vexed for a while. Don't try to change or push aside what they are experiencing.

Validating does not mean agreeing. The significant point is that you can acknowledge your partner's sentiments, yet it doesn't mean you have to agree with them. For example, think of when you go out to see a film together. A short time after you come back, you talk about your thoughts about the film. Your partner thought that it was engaging and clever, while you thought that it was boring and unsurprising. You may approve of their perspective by saying, "It sounds like you truly liked the film. It wasn't that good for me, but I can tell that you had a good time watching it." In this manner, you're validating your partner's satisfaction in something without having a similar opinion.

You should ask questions. If your partner relates an issue or troublesome circumstance to you, attempt to understand how they are feeling and what they need by asking some questions. "What do you wish for?" "What was your response to that?" "How are you feeling about things currently?" Gently posing these questions to elucidate their experience can be satisfying for them. It indicates that you gave it a second thought and tried to understand them.

Show that you get it. Utilize validating sentences—for example, "I would feel that way as well" or "It sounds good to me that you'd feel that way under these conditions"—to tell them that you see why they feel the way they do. You can likewise indicate validation with nonverbal methods—for example, giving them an embrace anytime that they feel forlorn, making them some tea if they feel anxious, or giving them space if they need time to think.

At last, it's about how you connect, considerably more so than what you do together. Furthermore, it can have a significant effect on your relationship.

Validation in Conflicts

Don't use invalidating sentences like the ones given below. These will lead to increased conflict and may intentionally or unintentionally cause a lot of hurt feelings.

- "You are too sensitive."
- "You're being ridiculous."
- "Stop overreacting. Lighten up."
- "Learn to take a joke."
- "Stop freaking out over everything."
- "Why are you always emotional?"
- "Don't be so irrational."
- "Get over it already!"
- "Don't get upset over silly things all the time."

- "Why do you even let it bother you?"
- "I don't want to deal with this drama again."
- "It's not even a big deal."

Go over this list again and remember not to use these sentences in the future. When you think about it, it's quite sobering. These simple words can hurt your partner and invalidate their feelings in a major way. You have probably used them a lot over the years, and it has done nothing to improve your relationship.

Validation can help you show real love and consideration for your partner. Even when you love them, invalidating behavior on your part will make it seem otherwise for them. This is why you need to understand and practice validation for yourself and your partner. Learn to acknowledge that their feelings and thoughts are equally as valid as yours even when they are different. Every individual has the right to have different opinions and feelings in a certain situation, and as a partner, it is important that you give them support and understanding.

Chapter 6: The Role and Importance of Empathy in Your Relationship

What Is Empathy?

People tend to confuse empathy with sympathy. However, it is important for you to know the difference between the two. To have compassion for someone means to feel pity or sorrow for them when they face some misfortune. To have empathy means to be able to understand and share their feelings.

It is not uncommon for people to disagree with each other on things. Everyone has their own opinions and feelings. However, it is important to respect the other person's feelings and not try to railroad over them with your own. This is especially so in a relationship. You have to cultivate a sense of compassion and endure the other person's views and emotions. Empathy will allow you to do this and develop a strong relationship with your partner.

Influence of Empathy in a Relationship

It is important for you to have empathy for your partner, and they should do the same for you too. When you can empathize with another person, you will be able to feel what they are feeling in some way. For instance, you will understand their pain or feel happy when they are happy. If you can develop empathy within yourself, you will be able to perceive your partner's emotions even as they keep changing. This is crucial in helping you both to understand each other and to provide support when they need it. Having empathy will help you become more compassionate. Developing compassion in yourself is important as it will make you want to help your partner in their time of need and provide them with the care they require. If you fail to have empathy for the other person, you will not be able to have compassion for them either. This is because you will fail to recognize their emotions and thus fail to react appropriately too. According to many studies, people who lack empathy are usually the ones who are mean to others. They fail to understand how their words and actions affect the other person. Such people lie to themselves and refuse to take responsibility for their actions. They rarely show remorse for hurting another person. These days, people get so wrapped up in themselves that they neglect developing empathy in their nature. This can have a negative effect on all their relationships in life regardless of whether it is at work or home.

Empathy is actually at the heart of a happy relationship. Your relationship will struggle to survive when it lacks empathy. You will lack compassion without empathy, and this will affect the bond you have with your partner. Empathy is like a bridge between two individuals who have different feelings, thoughts, or perspective. Empathy can be of three types.

- *Cognitive empathy* is when you can look at things from another person's perspective but cannot feel their emotions. It will allow you to appreciate a situation the other person is going through.

- *Emotional empathy* allows you to feel what the other person is feeling or thinking. It allows you to connect with the person more emotionally.
- *Compassionate empathy* is a balance of both cognitive and emotional empathy. It allows you to see things from the other person's perspective and empathize with their emotions as well.

Compassionate empathy is what you need to develop to a greater extent within yourself. Cognitive or emotional empathy can often have a negative impact. For instance, someone can use it to manipulate someone for their benefit. But with compassionate empathy, you will feel compassion and be less inclined to want to harm anyone. If you have compassionate empathy, you will think twice before you do anything and will be more considerate of your partner's feeling. If you know that your partner feels annoyed or frustrated when the room is messy, you will empathize and make an effort to keep it clean. Your empathy will help you become a good partner, and they will appreciate your efforts. Compassionate empathy will help you respond to your partner with love, compassion, and understanding.

How to Develop Empathy

Now that you recognize the importance of it, you should make an effort to nurture empathy within yourself. The following steps will help you in becoming more empathetic.

Increase your self-awareness. When you become more attuned to your own emotions and thoughts, you will also be able to recognize these in others. If something hurts you, you will know that it could hurt another person too. Take notice of how you feel and think when your partner is saying or doing something. Don't be too absorbed in yourself and learn to exert control over the way you react.

Practice self-empathy. You will fail to empathize with your partner when you cannot sympathize with yourself. You need to pay attention to your own emotions and acknowledge when you are going through a difficult time. Taking care of yourself should always be a priority. Don't compromise self-care in an attempt to take care of your partner. If you take care of yourself, you will be better able to care for them too. You can face your issues without catastrophic about it. Remaining calm and composed will help you meet everything that comes your way.

Pay attention to body language. Be careful about your body language and learn to observe that of others as well. A person's gestures, expressions, and various movements can tell a lot about their feelings.

Observe nonverbal cues. How a person says something is often more revealing than what they are saying. The nonverbal cues will help to identify their emotional truth.

Develop the habit of listening well. You won't be able to empathize with someone if you don't even listen to what they are saying. Pay attention to the details, and be a good listener. Avoid interrupting someone when they talk. Give them a chance to express themselves freely. Too many people are focused on talking more than listening. Give genuine attention to your partner at all times. Even when you argue, don't be focused on finding a way to defend yourself. Pay attention to what they are saying and try to understand their perspective.

Look for the positive aspects of your partner and your relationship. When you focus too much on the negative, you affect your ability to empathize healthily. Start taking note of the good things instead of constantly thinking of the bad.

Avoid being judgmental or doubting what the other person says. Listen with an open heart and mind. Don't focus too much on wanting to give advice or telling them what they should or should not do. When a person shared their problem, they trust you and are looking for support. You should be more focused on listening than trying to solve the problem.

Keep your own opinions and values aside and focus on what the other person feels and needs from you. Being too entangled in your perspective will prevent you from acting mindfully toward your partner.

Use these tips to develop a sense of empathy for your partner and others. It will make a lot of difference in the way you communicate with people, and it will positively improve your relationships with them.

How to Communicate with Empathy

Now that you understand a little more about empathy, you have to start communicating with it in mind. If you are someone who struggles with finding the right things to say, the following statements might help you figure it out.

Acknowledge your partner's pain. It is very important for you to acknowledge how they feel at all times. They will feel supported when you connect with their struggle or pain.

You may use the following sentences:

- "I am sorry that you have to go through this."
- "I hate that this happened to you."
- "I wish I could turn things around and make it easier for you."
- "This must be hard for you."
- "I can see that this must be a difficult situation for you."

Share your feelings. You can be truthful and admit it when you don't know what to say or do. It is not always easy to imagine what the other person is going through. Share your thoughts and let your partner know that you are trying.

You may use the following sentences:

- "I wish I could make things better."
- "My heart hurts for you."
- "I can't imagine how hard this must be for you."
- "I'm really sad that this happened to you."
- "I'm sorry that you are feeling this way."

Show your partner that you are grateful when they open up to you. People find it difficult to open up and be vulnerable to others. More often than not, their trust has been broken at some point. So when they choose to trust you, you need to be grateful and express it. Show your partner you appreciate that they share their thoughts and emotions with you. Acknowledge how difficult it can be for them to do this sometimes.

You may use the following sentences:

- "I'm glad that you shared this with me."
- "I'm glad that you are telling me this."
- "I can imagine how hard it must be to talk about this. Thank you for sharing it with me."
- "I appreciate you trying to work hard on our relationship. I know you are trying, and that gives me hope."
- "Thank you for trusting me and opening up. I want to be there for you."

Show your partner that you are interested.
You have to take an interest in what your partner is going through. It can be hard to go through difficult times alone. You have to reach out and show them that you are there for support. Show them that you are interested in listening to whatever they have to say. Don't offer too much advice or too many opinions. Just be a good listener.

You may use the following sentences:

- "I'm here for you if you want to talk."
- "How are you feeling about all that's been going on lately?"
- "Are you OK? Is there something you want to talk about?"
- "I think you're feeling like ——. Am I right? Did I misunderstand?"
- "What has this been like for you?"

Show encouragement. When your loved one is going through a tough time, you have to be encouraging. But you need to go about this the right way. Don't try to fix their problem or offer unsolicited advice. Just encourage them in a way that makes them feel better and motivated. Show them that you care and that you believe in them.

You may use the following sentences:

- "You are strong, and I believe you can get through this."
- "I am always on your side. You should never feel alone."
- "I'm proud of everything that you have done."
- "You matter, and you should never question it."
- "You are a very talented person."

Show support. Actions matter more than words at times. You can take some simple actions to show your partner you are there to support and help them through any tough times. You can send them flowers to make them feel better. You can do some chores for them. Just do anything that you feel they will appreciate, and that will make their life a little easier.

You may use the following sentences:

- "I want to do this for you."
- "I am always here to listen."
- "Is there anything I can do for you right now?"
- "Is there any way I can help?"
- "Tell me what you need."

But in the end, there is no fixed script when it comes to sympathy. You have to be more attuned to your partner's needs and act likewise. Half the work is just listening and being there for them. I hope the examples given here help you in dealing with such situations in a better and more empathetic way.

Show Your Partner You Appreciate Them

A lot of us tend to take our partners for granted over time. We love them, and we know that they do a lot for us. However, we fail to thank and appreciate them for all that they do for us. If you think about it, you probably do this as well. This is why I have dedicated this section to learn more about how to show appreciation to your partner.

A lot of you may shirk it off and say that you hate obvious or public displays of affection. You may say that you appreciate your partner and that they already know it, so there is no need to show it all the time. But this is where you are wrong. When you do something nice for your partner, would you like it better if they expressed their appreciation, or is it always enough that you know they appreciate it in their heart? Everyone needs a little show of affection and gratitude. It helps them feel good and happy when they see this extra effort from their partner. When you think of how you should behave with your partner, consider this: How would you want them to behave with you and treat you? And are you doing the same as well? This is always a general rule of thumb for everyone: "Do unto others as you would have them do unto you." You should treat people the way you want to be treated too. So if you would like a little more appreciation, why not do the same for your partner?

Grand romantic gestures usually get all the hype. They will be appreciated, but they are not all that important. The little gestures can play a much bigger role in the long run if you remember to be consistent in your efforts. If you make a point to keep showing your partner that you appreciate them, it will all add up. Sending a big bouquet once a year does not cut. The little gestures you make regularly will help in making your relationship even stronger because it will demonstrate the affection and commitment you have toward your partner.

In a lot of studies, couples have complained about the fact that they feel their partner does not appreciate them enough. They always feel like they put in a lot of effort for their partner but see no sign of recognition or acknowledgment for it. This can be frustrating and depressing for the partner and leaves them dissatisfied. Showing a little appreciation can go a long way. When you start showing your partner appreciation, you will find that you both are much happier together, and the love feels rekindled.

I feel, as individuals, we always want positive consideration. Furthermore, acknowledging somebody is the ideal approach to doing it. The issue begins when we don't see how we slipped into a habit of underestimating each other and quit thinking about and valuing each other. This prompts different issues—fights, dissatisfaction, and disdain. All of a sudden, we start to think about whether this relationship is ever going to work out.

How about we look at a basic (and most likely not very unprecedented) situation. Your partner dependably drops your kid(s) off to class. He or she has been doing it for some time now. Be that as it may, you never disclosed to them the amount you value them for it or recognized how grateful you are for it. Imagine a scenario in which he or she just stopped doing this one day. You would need to alter your very own calendar for it, likely begin getting up marginally earlier in the morning every day or quit viewing your preferred breakfast shows so that you can get ready to leave for work each day. What was a seemingly trivial thing all of a sudden ends up significant when it isn't being done anymore!

When I propose that couples begin building on the habit of expressing gratitude toward each other and valuing their partners for each seemingly insignificant detail they take care of, I am regularly met with a grimace or mocking looks. All things considered, what is the need to thank somebody for a vocation that they should do in any case just like everybody else? This, to me, is a real issue. What's more, a major one at that—one that most women have to face and suffer in gratitude for. It's an indication that you figure the things you do (or you trust you do) are not as significant as the easily overlooked details that your partner does. What's more, that is the place where the balance in a relationship seems to go off-scale.

Thankfulness is key to any relationship. Acknowledging somebody makes them like what they do and feel that it has any positive effect in their lives. It makes them rest easy thinking about themselves in a good way, allowing them to go on with new energy, reinforcing your relationship.

Things being what they are, how would you know when your partner feels unappreciated?

There are a few signs that will show that you might be underestimating the issues in your relationship and your partner feels undervalued hence:

- They get into fights over seemingly insignificant details.
- They have begun acting progressively emotional of late.
- They don't like talking to you as much as before.
- They don't want your opinion anymore.
- They make arrangements without counseling you.
- They are not excited about the special events they used to enjoy before.
- They don't endeavor toward pleasing you any longer.

- They seem distant from you.
- They might have an affair.

There are two angles to being appreciative—one depends on timing, and the other on core interest. Time-sensitive gratefulness is somewhat of a problem. With time, you either turned out to be increasingly irritated with your partner's conduct, or you become all the more tolerating. Precisely which way it swings out to will depend on your viewpoint.

Acceptance emerges from your understanding that things are not liable to change after some time, and subsequently, you become all the more tolerating. When you become more tolerant, you will think that it's simpler to acknowledge what they do. If you change your point of view, you may discover that even (what used to be) their most annoying habits may have some value. What's more, this enables you to concentrate on what makes your partner happier.

There are so many easy and simple ways to show your partner appreciation:

Smile at them. There is nothing simpler yet more effective than smiling at someone with love. Like I said before, verbal communication is only half the game, so a simple thank you is not always enough. Take time to look at your partner and smile at them from your heart. That one smile will show them that you feel grateful for what they do and the fact that they are in your lives. A smile can convey a lot without you having to say it out loud. It will barely take some seconds of your time to smile at your partner a few times every day.

Start paying attention. Don't listen to what your partner says with half an ear. Look them in the eye and turn toward them when they are talking to you. Show them that you are interested in what they are saying. Ask them how their day was. If they said they were craving food, remember and bring it for them the next day. Surprise them by showing that you pay attention to the little details. Show them that you care and that you think of them the way they are always thinking of you. They will appreciate it.

Show them that you are reliable. In a relationship, it is important that your partner can count on you. Both people need to be accountable for their actions and safe for each other. They should be assured of the fact that their partner will keep their word and honor their promises. Don't betray your partner's trust and make sure that they know they can depend on you at all times. Don't be late when you're supposed to meet them. Don't forget something they asked you to do. Be reliable the way they are for you. If you want them to support you, you should give them some as well.

Physical gestures of affection. Physical affection is powerful. Holding their hands, hugging them, or just a simple peck on the cheek can make so much difference. Don't hold out on your affection and be free with it; your partner deserves it. It reinforces the sense of love and romance in your relationship. Squeeze their hands to show them support. Give them a long hug whenever you can.

Be thankful. Learning to say "Thank you" is probably one of the first few things we all learn as children. This is because everyone knows the importance of expressing appreciation to others when they do something for you. There is very little effort required to say "Thank you," but you will get numerous opportunities throughout the day to say it. Don't stop thanking your partner just because they do the same thing for you every day. Instead, start thanking them every day and show that you genuinely appreciate their effort. Say "Thank you" when they hand you a cup of coffee and say "Thank you" even when they ask you about your day. How many people care about how your day went other than your partner?

Be helpful. You have to thank them and appreciate them for all that they do. However, it is not enough to be thankful all the time; you have to make an effort to do things for them as well. If you have time, do a chore for them. Go for the grocery run or make dinner. Help them complete their work. Do things to help them and show that you know they work hard.

Make small sacrifices. If your partner realizes you detest peas with a fierceness sufficiently able to fuel a fly plane yet you make them in any case, that is the sort of little compromise that demonstrates you think about their wants and needs. The purpose of such small sacrifices is to explain to your partner that you value them enough to put their needs and wants in front of your own occasionally. In a progressively self-centered world, this is an extreme demonstration of unselfishness that indicates gratefulness, benevolence, and love.

I'm certain your partner would likewise welcome a surprise gift or some special gesture. In any case, in general, some portion of being a decent partner is figuring out how to demonstrate your thankfulness in the seemingly insignificant details and in little ways every day.

Repairing and Regaining Trust

The Importance of Trust

Trust is an essential element in a happy and healthy relationship. In a good relationship, both people will have complete trust over each other. This is because they feel safe with each other and know they can depend on the other person for love and support throughout. This is especially so in a marriage or any intimate relationship. However, as humans, we are prone to mistakes, and this can often cause the other person to lose trust in us. This could happen due to a variety of reasons. The trust between partners is usually damaged severely in case of infidelity or any significant lies. Breaking promises is another cause of mistrust. This is not about small white lies or a silly promise. It is about the big ones that involve important matters. For instance, if your partner confided in you and shared a big secret, it will damage their trust in you if you share that secret with others. This is why you need to be more careful about such things.

One of the worst ways to lose your partner's trust is to cheat on them. Infidelity is usually a deal breaker in most relationships. More often than not, this is not a mistake that they will be willing to forgive or forget. However, if they are willing to stay in the relationship with you and work on it, you need to give it your best. Winning back someone's trust can be much harder the second time around. At first, people are more open and likely to open up and trust a person. However, if they feel betrayed, they will be wary and unwilling to trust someone again. This is why you need to acknowledge your mistake and put in all the effort required to regain their trust. Your relationship can be salvaged if you both are completely committed to getting past this phase. There are various steps involved in the process of rebuilding trust in a relationship, and each of these is equally important.

Steps to Rebuild Trust

As a couple, you both need to listen to each other properly and hear what the other person has to say. You need to have an open discussion about the betrayal that has caused this issue. Also, remind each other that you both need and deserve honest and open answers to any questions if you have to get past this.

If a particular situation has caused one partner to lose trust in the other, there has to be an open discussion on it. The offender needs to be forthcoming about all the details and be honest with their partner. You both have to understand that there are two sides to every story. You both need to talk about it and try to understand the situation with more clarity. Talk about what happened and when or where it happened. Try to find the reason why this kind of situation arose in the first place. Be open about your feelings and thoughts to each other. You will often see the situation in a different way when you do all this. Seeing the offender's perspective and hearing an honest narrative will provide clarity to the other partner. The offending partner will also get a better understanding of how their actions have affected the other person.

A situation that causes loss of trust in a relationship will also give rise to a lot of anger. Anger builds and destroys the person that always holds it in. So you both need to release your anger healthily. Don't let it fester and harm you. In such situations, you both may find it difficult to sleep, stay calm, or even lose appetite. Irritability is common, and the smallest incidents can trigger a negative reaction. Don't try to hold the anger in. It will not benefit you or your relationship. You both need to think about your feelings and understand why you are feeling this way. It is OK to express your anger with each other. If one has betrayed the other's trust, they have to be willing to accept the feelings of resentment and anger their actions have caused. The offending partner may also be angry due to other reasons and should express their feelings as well. It is important to release the anger for it to dissipate.

If you betray your partner in any way, they will question your commitment to the relationship. You will do the same if they betray your trust. This is why it is important to take actions and express yourself in a way that shows real commitment to the relationship. If you fail to show commitment, they might even reconsider working or staying in this relationship. You have to give validation to your partner's feelings and thoughts if you have betrayed their trust. Show them that you accept your mistake and acknowledge the part you have played in this situation. You can share your feelings as well and let them know that you are committed to getting past this and improving your situation. If you are the one who betrayed their trust, show remorse and let them know that you want to make it up to them. You both have to let each other know what your expectations are from each other and this relationship in the future. These clear expectations should be met with a willingness from both sides to fulfill them. You and your partner have to tell each other what you are not OK with and what might trigger conflict in the future. This will let both partners know what they need to avoid and be careful of if they want their relationship to work.

Both partners have to make a conscious decision to let go of the past. This means that they each have to be willing to forgive and be forgiven by the other. Forgiving someone is easier said than done. However, if you are willing and give it time, it is possible. Forgiveness will require commitment and effort from both your parts.

After discussing the situation, you both should be able to identify the various underlying causes. To avoid any such issue in the future, you have to work on self-improvement and personal growth. If you betrayed your partner, you have to work on yourself and be better. Don't make any empty promises and show your commitment to real actions. If your partner sees you put in the work and grow as a person, they will be more willing to trust in you again. If you make any promises to them, you have to follow through.

You both should stop obsessing about the situation. There is no point in continuously thinking of it and pondering over it. Instead, express your thoughts and feelings to each other. Being open with each other and discussing such things will prevent anger and resentment from festering. You have to be true and show that you want and intend to work on this relationship.

If you want to repair the trust in your relationship and recover from this negative phase, all of these above-mentioned points have to be kept in mind.

Chapter 7: Dealing with Infidelity

Infidelity or having an affair can be especially challenging to get over in a relationship. It shakes the foundation of your partnership or marriage and will make your partner feel completely betrayed. If you are both still willing to get over it and heal your relationship, you need to find the underlying cause of it. Many reasons can lead to an affair. The following are some of the most commonly identifiable ones:

- The partner wants physical intimacy that they are not receiving from their marriage. A lot of marriages face issues when there is a lack of sexual relations between the two partners. Hence, it may drive one of them to seek it elsewhere.

- A partner feels underappreciated in their relationship. They look for another person who might give them more attention and appreciate them.

- There is too much fighting or bickering in the relationship.
- They want some more excitement back in their lives and their monotonous marriage fails to provide it.
- A partner might also cheat to seek revenge for some reason.
- Some cheat to boost their ego and sense of self-worth by seeing that someone else still finds them attractive.
- The person feels trapped in the relationship.
- Some partners might have an affair if it will help them combat some difficult situation, such as financial issues.
- Sex addiction can also lead to multiple affairs.
- Some cheat only for the experience of a one-night stand.
- They might also cheat after they experience some trauma and want to escape the situation and their emotional state.

You can both discuss and see if any of these are the underlying cause for the adultery done by you or your partner. More often than not, you will be able to relate to one or more of these reasons.

If you are the person who betrayed your partner's trust, you have to be willing to accept the consequences of your actions. Don't shy away from apologizing and validating the impact your actions have had on the relationship. You have to show a change in your actions and behavior to your partner if you want to regain their trust. Don't expect them to forgive you and trust in you again based on some empty promises and an apology. A real change in your behavior will make them trust that you will not betray them again. You need to stop keeping secrets and lying, no matter what. Be more open and forthcoming with them. Transparency is crucial if you want it to work. Also, be honest when they ask you questions about why or how something happened. If you lied, let them know why you did. Don't try to shirk off their questions, and instead, be honest. It will allow you both to get to the root of whatever the real issue is. Don't be defensive and try to salvage your ego. You have to take responsibility for your actions in this case as well as at other times. Don't try to justify your behavior or push the blame on your partner. Such words and actions will only perpetuate the situation.

The person who was betrayed also plays an important role in this. If your trust was broken or you feel betrayed by your partner, you have to decide if it is something you can forgive and get past. If you are committed to working on your relationship, then you have to participate in the effort it will require to rebuild the trust between you both. It is important that you ask your partner any questions you have and try to understand the situation better. You need to identify the underlying causes of all these issues. These things will not justify your partner's betrayal, but it will help you move past it sooner. If your partner is showing remorse and is trying hard to gain your trust again, help them out a little.

Let them know what you need and how you feel. Give them feedback on what will positively set you both on the right track again. They won't know what you want or need if you don't say anything. If anything about their behavior or habits bothers you, let them know and suggest improvements. You should also be willing to listen to their side and accommodate some of their needs if they are reasonable and in the best interest of the relationship. However, if you feel like the betrayal was too great and unforgivable, it is OK. You have the prerogative to say you are unwilling to remain in the relationship anymore. There are certain situations where the trust really cannot be regained. But if you feel like it can, I hope the advice given in this chapter is of some help in the process.

A couple that is working on rebuilding trust has to understand that it is like starting all over again. You have to make an effort to win over the other person and show real commitment to them. You both need to be expressive and honest with each other. Don't expect that your partner will know what you want without you saying anything. You should both put in work and try to reestablish a supportive connection that will allow the relationship to flourish again. Show that you appreciate your partner and love them.

If you both find it too hard to work on all this yourself, you can consider professional help. Couple counseling or even single counseling sessions can be extremely helpful and has helped salvage a lot of relationships. Find a counselor that you can trust and has a good reputation. A therapist will help you work through the process and actively get past this current phase in your relationship. No matter how you do it, you and your partner have to understand the importance of trust in a relationship and not take it for granted again.

Chapter 8: Relationship Affirmations

Affirmations are one of the easiest yet most effective ways to use the law of attraction in your favor. If you want your relationship to be strong and happy, you truly have to believe that it will be. Repeating these affirmations to yourself daily will push these positive thoughts to the universe. It will help in making it all come true and establishing a good foundation for your relationship no matter how many struggles you go through.

- "My relationship is growing strong every single day."
- "My partner loves and encourages me all the time."
- "The foundation of my relationship is trust and loyalty."
- "My partner and I are completely in love."
- "My relationship is nothing short of a miracle."
- "My partner loves me unconditionally."

- "My partner and I help each be a better version of ourselves."
- "Every day our relationship gets strong, and we will always work hard to keep it that way."
- "My relationship is a gift from God."
- "We have a powerful and passionate relationship."
- "My partner is the perfect person for me, and I will accept them wholeheartedly."
- "We are both faithful to each other at all times."
- "My partner and I shower each other with love and affection."
- "My relationship will never be tainted with hate, lies, anger or hurt."
- "Our relationship will stand the test of time."
- "Our relationship is blessed with love, compassion, loyalty, and abundance."

Remember to repeat these affirmations every day and with complete faith in them. You will soon see it all being manifested in your relationship.

Avoiding Fights, Communicating through Conflicts, and Finding Solutions

If you are reading this, it is safe to say that you are in a relationship and tend to fight a lot.

Relationships are tied in with loving and fighting. But more often than not, it tends to be "your friends are so inappropriate" fight, "I can't read your mind" fight, etc. Either partner will always be looking for an opening to criticize and fight with the other even when they love each other. However, have you, at any point, seen these kinds of couples stop and think in the manner that, despite everything, they have to remain by each other's side?

In the end, no fight bodes well for your relationship. It will be about how well you proceed onward from that fight and begin everything all over again.

Along these lines, to all the battling and contending couples out there, this is something that I need to let you know. It's OK not to agree with each other all the time. Furthermore, here are some important pointers

115

you ought to recall when you are in this kind of relationship.

Everyone Wants an Ideal Relationship

"I need him to hold my hand when we go out." "I need her to quit looking at different young men." "I wish to have a partner who is like this." "I wish my partner would sometimes do this." We need the grinning, kissing, snickering, and holding. We need everything. Indeed! We figure it will always be similar to how it is in the honeymoon phase.

Be that as it may, when we get into a genuine relationship, we understand that it isn't what we figured it ought to be. We get baffled, we get irate, we feel slighted, and we end up being disappointed by the truth of a relationship. The reality is, in case you're genuinely in a relationship, you have to make a few trade-offs and need to make a few concessions. But the uplifting news is that fights can be great.

As indicated by many studies, the couples that argue or fight the most adore each other the most as well.

The facts demonstrate that arguments in a relationship can help improve it; however, like everything else, balance is necessary. One should know the contrast between necessary and superfluous arguments. In addition, in case you're truly going to fight, remember that there are a few reasonable methods of doing it.

Presently, we will perceive how fighting is useful for a relationship.

1. **Fighting fortifies the relationship.** When we fight or we contend, we genuinely uncover our true selves before our partner. Along these lines, they become acquainted with the genuine us. They realize what sort of person we are and what feelings we convey. They are a learning experience where, however many injuries we face, it makes us greater and stronger with time.

2. **By fighting, the couple communicates.** We all realize that fighting can draw out the most exceedingly terrible parts in us. In any

case, did you at any point believed that it could likewise draw out the best of us? When we fight, we attempt our best to convey what needs be said, and that is the thing that a relationship calls for. When you state, "I don't care for when you do X," in any event, your partner will be able to comprehend that the thing is critical to you.

3. ***Fighting upgrades the relationship rationally.*** It builds closeness. By fighting, we become more acquainted with what is significant for our partner, what they don't care for, what they need, where their limits are, what they are willing to adjust to, what tends to hurt them, and what they need be improved. As per research, this increases the closeness and comprehension between partners in a relationship.

4. ***We learn they are a different person.*** In the wake of being with somebody for quite a while, we think they know us, they get us, and above all, they are agreeable around us. Be that

118

as it may, it is true that, when we fight, we come to realize how much was hidden from us.

5. *Fighting will allow you to improve.* According to studies, after a fight takes place, one begins dealing with the things that disturb the other. We increment our understanding, care, and love for our other half.

You are human. Don't endeavor to be flawless! Everybody loses their mind. Everybody has uncertain issues. Everybody experiences awful states of mind. Once a while, everybody feels powerless. This demonstrates you're human. Quit trying to be flawless like some people seemingly are since it is OK not to be OK now and again.

What you have to remember is that you need to consider your partner's perspective. For once, attempt to place yourself in the shoes of your partner. Nothing will be explained if you don't listen to their point of view. One needs to comprehend that his or her view isn't the absolute fact at all times; there are a lot progressively elective points of view. If you are receptive, you could gather their perspectives. Attempt and comprehend. The significant aphorism is that both of you should be willing, and for this, it is critical to see things from each other's perspective.

It is essential to move on after a fight has passed. Always remember, there is no love without absolution, and there is no pardoning without affection!

How to Avoid Fighting with Your Partner

From one viewpoint, how you want the outcome of an argument with a partner or loved one to be depends on how you perceive it in your mind and, along these lines, can be under your control. So one answer for avoiding fights is to build up your day-by-day meditation practice in which you figure out how to remove yourself from negative thoughts that sort of push you toward a fight with your partner. You will learn to see that those thoughts are simply just thoughts, not strong proclamations speaking to "reality." They become like mist in the sky—here one minute, gone the following. They may glide above you for some time; however, you shouldn't harp on them or pay attention to them. Overseeing your mind through contemplation practice is one approach to prevent fights; however, it is an individual undertaking, and fighting takes at least two individuals.

Discussing a fight with your partner is another way and one that can improve your entire relationship; it's a two-person issue and a two-person arrangement. Fights that build up are quite often the consequence of the cycle of blame and outrage (or even anger, as certain analysts call it, even though that may be hyper-emotional). Let's take a gander at a precedent; this is what occurs. You said you'd accomplish something, and you neglected to do it. Your partner neglects the fact that you were quite busy yesterday and it's reasonable that it escaped your attention. Rather, your partner turns on you with allegations that you are continually overlooking things, breaking your promises, or not pulling your weight. Your partner may even unobtrusively show that you are a languid person who expects everything to be given to you on a gold platter. You take in this character assassination, and even though you would prefer not to trust it, you dread—under the dimension of cognizant mindfulness—that the person might be correct and that you merit the fault being stacked upon you.

Your guard goes up like a piece of the marble wall, and to stop that repulsive on-edge feeling that we call *coerce*—a dread that you've harmed somebody (for this situation your partner)—you turn it around. You "externalize" (to utilize the word clinicians use), and you argue that the circumstance was in actuality your partner's issue because they left you no opportunity to get your work together or they are continually pushing repetitive errands on you rather than assuming liability themselves. You then start the process of character assassination yourself, telling your partner this is run of the mill, that they are negligent, harsh, and in a general sense, a narrow-minded individual. So the fault is tossed back, and your partner, similar to you, tunes down and trusts each word you state. They can't stand feeling so much blame and turn it around yet again, externalizing (i.e., making you the culprit once more). Thus it goes, forward and backward, with no possibility of being resolved. This is why the blame game is a never-ending negative cycle for your relationship.

The beneficial thing here is that you can intrude on the cycle without letting your partner know. When a fight breaks out, stop for a minute and enable yourself to perceive that you feel as remorseful as though you'd carried out wrongdoing (probably a nonexistent one). Perceive the blame. Feel it. However, don't pay attention to it (mindful reflection can be useful here). At that point, think about some approach to abstain from accusing your partner consequently. A push to forgo externalizing and accusing the other will make a quick break on the circumstance. The fight will end, your vitality will be saved, and maybe you and your partner will most likely examine the contentious issue later on. Commonly, the focal point of this fight is a misrepresentation of everyday life issues at any rate. Record—in basic language—the core of the issue. It's regularly about the allotment of errands or cash. Or on the other hand, possibly you and your partner have been fighting, with an aggressive edge, about how much space both of you take up at get-togethers. In the cool light of day, the dispersion of the family expenses might be considered and arranged effectively; the same remains constant for the portion of cash and for sharing consideration in a social circumstance.

You probably won't most likely stop the following fight with your partner, yet you will almost certainly step further from it and inspect it, taking note of the fault of the blame cycle. When you can see this cycle working in a genuine situation, you'll have the option to change your style or strategies while fighting. When you abstain from accusing your partner, the person in question will calm down rapidly and forgo accusing you back. Furthermore, you will see the cycle, I promise you. It is to be anticipated; it's a law of a two-person framework.

What Not to Do after Fighting with Your Partner

Try not to treat them with utter disdain. If you need some space after a fight, that is fine, as long as you let them know. One of the greatest oversights individuals make after they fight is stonewalling. On the off chance that you get over your partner or overlook them, they may believe you're rebuffing them, which may make them keep down on disclosing to you how they feel later on. Rather, state, "My feelings don't pass off as fast as yours, so you need to allow me twenty-four hours, and I will be fine. If not, we can discuss this some more."

Try not to keep their words as ammunition for later. Do you know of the saying, "What happens in Vegas remains in Vegas"? Whatever your partner says amid a fight should remain there. So if they say something during the fight that bugs you, disclose to them that their words are confusing you. In case their words need defending and bother you, the following day, give yourself some breathing room as opposed to moving toward them again so soon. Raising an argument again can prompt conversations nonsensically, not a solution.

Don't simply say, "I'm hurt" if despite everything they're hurt. Instead of saying, "I'm tired of this. Disregard me. I need to accomplish something different," what you need to state is, "I'm upset for . . ." and clarify what you're discussing. The second piece of the statement of regret is "Later on, I will . . ." And fill in the blank with how you won't commit the error once more.

Try not to rationalize why you fought. There are a million things on which you could blame a fight: an awful day at work, a headache, and a tiring night. It has been found that couples that don't get enough rest are bound to fight. Passing the accusations around isn't reasonable for you or your partner. In case you're irate, upset, or hurt, that is something your better half has to know. When you have a terrible day at work, send a message to let your partner know before you return home. That way, they realize that you might be progressively crabby.

Try not to walk off because you're afraid that they might re-approach the fight. If it's been just a couple of minutes since your fight, advise your partner that you're open to any questions or additional complaints that they have had time to think about. In case they need to return to the issue following a couple of days, however, don't walk out on them. Nonverbal communication is as loud and obvious as shouting. If you wind up leaving, apologize, return, and listen to them. Reflect on what they are trying to let you know: "So you're saying ——, right?" Check in to ensure you're handling it right.

Try not to keep poking at them. You might still be reeling from a fight. That doesn't give you the privilege to murmur rude things under your breath. Never call your partner ugly names. It's difficult to recoup from that. So if you quarreled over your expenses, don't comment on how they're shabby in their photographs from the trip they took. Verbally abusing will make the other person return swinging with another insult. Rather, request that you resume talking once you've quieted down. Say something like, "I realize you're concerned we don't have the cash, yet here's a reasonable budget I made."

Try not to have sex after a fight in case you're not feeling it. You both said, "I'm grieved," and implied it. However, at this point, they're trying to get some, and all you can think is, "Seriously?" It isn't so difficult that they don't understand you fought. Numerous men need to engage in sexual relations to feel close to their partner again. If grinding away is the last thing at the forefront of your thoughts, let him down delicately. Just say, "Thank you for feeling like you need to be near me. However, I'm not in the temperament at present." Embrace him and reveal to him that you could engage in sexual relations the next day when you feel better.

Don't simply move over and deny them without clarification. That can be offending for your partner.

Try not to concentrate on what caused the fight. You can spend your energy better on the answers to the problem at hand. Think of this precedent: Say your partner neglected to pay a bill. You had a tiff about it, yet then you went to an ATM, paid the bill, and the issue was settled. Appreciate the night as opposed to replaying your partner's mistake up in your head. The distinction between a terrible fight and a decent fight is whether you achieved a resolution. Then again, if their absent-mindedness is consistent, have a go at saying, "I'm seeing that you aren't getting things done on time nowadays. What's happening there?" It's a less judgmental approach to get at the issue than "Ugh! Not once more!"

Try not to say, "I didn't mean it that way." Saying this is like trying to utilize an eraser on the indelible marker. It escalates the circumstance because your significant other will say, "Yes, you did!" "Going forward and backward on what you said or didn't say will keep you concentrated on the past as opposed to moving in the direction of an answer for the future, which is the objective of any argument. If they say, "I didn't mean it," say, "You didn't mean it, yet the outcome was that I felt hurt. So from now on, kindly do [XYZ]."

Try not to berate yourself over the fact that you fought. Everybody needs a partner who's contributing—and fighting can be an indication that you're both still working at the relationship (a positive thing!). A couple is destined to be together when they state, "We used to fight a great deal. However, at this point, we raise our hands and exit." It's not that they don't differ on things. It implies they're releasing control over the relationship, which is the thing that occurs before they leave or discover an undertaking. So feel great that you both still have consideration enough to get to the base of your issues.

How to Fight with Your Partner in a Healthy Way

With regard to relationships, the struggle is unavoidable. Be that as it may, it doesn't need to be genuinely troubling or insensitive. Couples can differ and truly even fight while still appearing and regarding each other.

Indeed, clinical therapist Deborah Grody says that wedded couples that don't have any quarrels are frequently the ones that end in separation. Relationships that can't be saved are relationships where the fire has totally gone out, or it wasn't there in any case, she says. When one or the two partners feel detached from their relationship, they couldn't care sufficiently enough to try to fight, as indicated by Grody.

Always having a heated and terrible fight is surely not beneficial or reasonable, either. You can effectively have some clash with your partner, and it might unite you, as indicated by a 2012 paper distributed by the

Society for Personality and Social Psychology. Specialists found that communicating outrage to a sentimental partner caused the momentary inconvenience of displeasure, yet in addition, it led to fair discussions that were beneficial for the relationship over the long haul.

If you need to explore fights with your partner in a more advantageous and progressively gainful way, remember these things the next time you are in an argument:

Be Interested in Your Fight

During sessions, Noam Ostrander, a partner teacher of social work at DePaul University, regularly asks couples, "What does the 5:30 fight resemble on weekdays?"

"They kind of grin since they know," says Ostrander. That is on the grounds that couples regularly fight over the same thing without settling anything, he says.

A typical reason for "the 5:30 fight," Ostrander says, is one partner feels the need to educate the other concerning their day and the other partner dodges it, requiring a moment to relax after returning home from work. This probably prompts one partner blaming the other for not thinking about them and the other partner feeling harassed.

Rather, Ostrander urges couples to pinpoint what triggers this redundant fight, and evaluate approaches to compromise as opposed to enabling the fight to escalate. Instead of following a similar old pattern, see that you don't fight when one partner just returns home, and propose another path around that.

"You can say, 'Imagine a scenario in which we simply stop, make proper conversation or kiss hi, allow it fifteen minutes, and return together,'" Ostrander says. Along these lines, the two-partners can impart that they would like to catch wind of the other individual's day and, together, locate the ideal approach to do that.

Pick a Time for Arguments

Regardless of having even the most open lines of communication, clashes are always bound to occur. What's more, when they do, it's useful to pick an opportunity to talk through issues, as indicated by Grody. If you begin to fight, say, "How about we bring it up tonight or some other time when there's an ideal opportunity to talk about things?"

Putting aside time to work out differences permits the two partners the space to regroup and get ready, Grody clarifies. They can consider sharing their emotions in a more settled and levelheaded way to achieve their goal of understanding each other. More often than not, foul things are said on purpose simply out of annoyance. In any case, the words remain with us long after they are said.

Take a Break if You or Your Partner Needs One

When in a fight, it's basic for one or the two partners to enter into a fight, flight, or freeze mode. People enter one of these modes when they figure they might be at risk. Fight or flight comes into the function when stress hormones are initiated to give individuals more energy to either fight the stressor causing stress or keep running from the circumstance. What's more, the other mode happens when an individual essentially does not respond by any means, with the expectation that the stressor loses enthusiasm for the fight.

At the point where a couple is in this dubious zone, mindful thinking is profoundly improbable because every individual is exclusively centered on responding to the apparent danger they feel from their partner. What's more, if just a single individual is in the fight, flight, or freeze mode while the other is endeavoring to determine the issue, it can disappoint the two individuals and heighten the fight.

In case you're truly annoyed with somebody and they're trying to ignore the issue, it can feel like they're not in any case listening. I believe sometimes people need to take a break.

Also, you can outline this break in a manner that doesn't make your partner feel like you're essentially leaving. Maybe someone says, "OK, I need to have this discussion. I need like ten minutes to quiet down. I love you. I'm not leaving," or, "We're going to talk about this. We're going to make sense of it."

When coming back to the discourse after some rest, the two individuals will be in an excellent spot to achieve genuine understanding.

Make Demands Rather Than Objections

Quarrels regularly begin with the usual two words: "You generally." Rather than asking that their partner to do something they'd like them to do, such as tidying up around the house, individuals tend to make allegations.

You're not getting what you need, given how you're asking it. It's simpler for individuals to ask their partner for a good reason for why they never accomplish something than it is just to demand that they do it.

Saying, "I'm not feeling well. I'm worried about how the house looks. Would you mind cleaning up some stuff?" is more straightforward and deferential than putting your cherished one down for his or her inability to address your issue. It's additionally bound to result in your partner finishing the assignment.

Listen and approach your partner for clarification.

At the point where the opportunity arrives to plunk down and discuss unraveling fights, the most significant thing couples can do is to listen without interfering. This can be surprisingly testing. If your partner says that the person in question doesn't feel heard, for instance, you ought to listen until your partner is done talking. At that point, ask for clarification if there is something you don't exactly get.

Asking, "What makes you feel like I'm not being attentive?" is a considerably more thoughtful approach to address your partner's grumbling than essentially saying, "Great, I'm tuning in, so you should feel heard." Reaching out and turning your body toward your partner when the individual in question is talking will likewise demonstrate that you are giving due attention to them. These little changes can avoid random fights in the future.

Also, obviously, amid any fight, put-downs and character assassination ought to be refrained from, no matter what. When it comes to the heart of the matter where there's verbal abusing and things like that, the dialogue should stop. It won't go anyplace. Couples can return to the discussion when the two people have had room to calm down.

Get familiar with the correct method to apologize to your partner.

Similarly, as individuals have distinctive ways to express affection, Ostrander says we have a diverse statement of regret dialects as well. It's insufficient to perceive that you've harmed your cherished one and you owe them a statement of regret. You need to know them enough to tailor your expression of remorse to their preference, as per Ostrander.

"A few people need enormous gestures, and a few people just need, 'I'm extremely sorry I offended you, and I will make sure not to do that once more,'" says Ostrander. "The procedure is making sense of what's important for your partner."

Expressing Yourself When You're Upset

Individuals frequently disclose to me that they have issues keeping up quiet and mindful conversations with their partner although they planned to. They begin fine yet can't finish when their partner reacts in impolite or irate ways. A number of these couples need the nearness of an accomplished relationship advisor to have the option to keep up quiet and fix disturbances.

This section offers a communication model that plots how to work on keeping up conversations concerning how you feel legitimately and openly while keeping your calm. This isn't tied in with feeling better or even agreeable. This is tied in with working on remaining quiet even though you feel hurt and irate.

The method of reasoning for this is having a full comprehension of each other's viewpoints. Feeling irate doesn't imply that you will undoubtedly separate. It implies that there is something you have to deal with.

If you figure out how to discover arrangements together, you will feel nearer, more secure, and comprehended on a more profound dimension. Envision disclosing to your partner that you are harmed and furious in a quiet manner. Additionally, envision that your partner can hear you and react in an adoring manner.

Since it is simpler to express positive sentiments and discussion about what's directly in your relationship, I will suggest that you begin with five positive explanations about yourself, your partner, and your relationship.

- What do you cherish about your partner?
- What do you cherish about the relationship?

- What is most critical to you?
- Give a solid case of what makes you feel cherished.
- Give a solid case of what you anticipate.

Communicate your adoration and gratefulness. Your ability to remain associated as well as to discover arrangements together is basic for your partner's eagerness to listen to you and think about your offers and proposed answers for issues you are having.

Chapter 9: Get a Therapist

Communicating feelings of disappointment, outrage, dread, and trouble is much harder and takes more time. If you can remain quiet and gathered while you talk about your feelings, your odds of staying on track are higher. If you abstain from accusing your partner and rather talk about what you feel and think and what is essential to you and why, almost certainly, your partner will react emphatically.

Make an effort to make it simpler for your partner to hear you out. Attempt to express your thoughts clearly to your partner. This is presumably one of the hardest activities. Self-articulation is tied in with characterizing yourself and what is most important to you. This is not simple when you are feeling disturbed and harmed.

It is normal in a relationship to feel on occasion that the other individual is to be faulted. In any case, if you think about the issue, you will end up mindful that you have an obligation regarding your very own reactions and responses, and how you work as a partner has an impact on the relationship. Your sentiments are your own, and to censure others for them isn't conducive for your individual or relationship development.

Before you begin communicating sentiments of indignation and hurt, I suggest that you consider what you are going to state and how you are going to state it. Think about the following:

What are your emotions? Do you feel furious, hurt, tragic, frightened, desolate, desirous or blameworthy?

Give solid models—for example, "I feel terrified when you don't call."

Concentrate more on what you feel, think, and need, not on your partner's weaknesses—for example, "I feel sad, and I miss what we used to do together."

Explain to your partner why you want to express your emotions sincerely and straightforwardly. Ensure you clarify that self-articulation goes in two different ways and that it takes bravery to discuss feeling defenseless. Hinting at vulnerabilities is a quality, and talking honestly about how you feel isn't a shortcoming.

Be aware of how you convey what needs be—manner of speaking, outward appearances, nonverbal communication, and eye contact. Be open and express what you want from the discussion.

On the off chance that you are exceptionally irate, you may feel vindictive. If that that is simply the situation, stay quiet and think about what is most essential to you and what sort of partner you might want to be.

Try not to anticipate prompt achievement. Self-articulation is an ability that takes practice to master. Ask for professional advice if you have to.

Below are the tips to help you control your emotions and express yourself in a better way.

Give Yourself Some Space

In my personal experience, one of the greatest mistakes I've done in a relationship is immediately lashing out to my partner when I am hurt without giving it much thought. For instance, I've lashed out in displeasure before truly knowing the other side of the story. This sort of lashing out will quite often create a feeling of defensiveness in the other person, and it hinders the progression of open and loving communication.

In this way, set aside some effort to truly feel what you are feeling and observe the necessities (and conceivably the unintegrated shadow angles) that are driving them.

Continuously Use Discernment

After you've set aside the effort to completely comprehend what you are feeling and why you are feeling it, it is critical to recognize whether speaking with somebody is extremely significant. When you give yourself space to completely process your feelings, you may find that it isn't really important to talk it through with the other individual. You may find that your emotions had nothing to do with the other individual.

Share with Trustworthy People

On the off chance that you conclude that you do need to ostensibly express your feelings, make sure that you do as such with individuals who have earned the privilege to your defenselessness.

Individuals who treat you like trash when you are open to them have not earned the privilege to hear your accounts. It is important to support relationships where it feels like a two-way road, where you both have considerations about the other individual's needs, wants, and sentiments without tiptoeing into codependency. This is important in order to feel satisfied with your relationships.

If you wind up rehashing examples of an unfortunate relationship (for example, being abused, disparaged, or controlled), then you can learn from their mistakes.

Learn to Speak with Clarity, Sympathy, and Empathy

If you have done the majority of the above-mentioned steps and are prepared to express your emotions to someone else, I prescribe a technique called nonviolent communication.

More or less, nonviolent communication (a.k.a. NVC) is a technique of communication that is based on the possibility that each activity is an attempt to address an issue. When we don't know viable systems for gathering our requirements, we resort to "brutality," which can look like hostility, hollering, accusing, and in the most pessimistic scenarios, perilous demonstrations of physical violence.

As I referenced in the main point, you should initially comprehend your feelings before you can utilize this way to express your emotions, and it might feel somewhat clumsy at first. We simply aren't instructed how to impart our necessities without fault, ultimatums, or requests; thus, it feels somewhat remote. In any case, it is quite worth that time of uneasiness to have the option to convey affectionately.

Assume Liability for Your Needs

We are social creatures (which is more surprising than being mutually dependent), which means we won't flourish without others helping us in our requirements. Be that as it may, when all is said and done, it is dependent upon you to guarantee that you feel satisfied in your life.

When you influence offers to someone else, do it without fault, ultimatums, or requests. In all probability, the other individual needs you to feel your best and will be pleased to help you with your requirements and qualities.

In any case, when you express your sentiments, recall that it isn't their business to do as such. They generally reserve the privilege to decline your offer, and it will be dependent upon you to make sense of approaches to get those requirements met without their assistance.

Be Patient with Yourself and Others

As I have mentioned before, a majority of us are not taught how to talk to others in a confident and appropriate way. If you feel you have been conveying your thoughts and emotions to others in the wrong way, you need to accept that it will take some time to get familiar with the new ways of communication.

In this way, if there is someone in particular that you feel you have communication issues with, make an effort to understand them and yourself first.

Having a child's mentality will help you. Don't anticipate that you or another person will be able to communicate better instantly. It will require some time and effort to unlearn the majority of the bad communication habits that you have learned over the years.

I cannot ensure that you will always be patient and can remain unresentful toward others. However, patience will make things much easier for you and them. What I know without a doubt, however, is that learning how to be more patient and kind in your communication will help you establish healthier relationships.

Chapter 10: Transform New Communication Skills into Healthy Mindful Habits

How to Master Mindful Communication

Applying mindful communication was nearly completely non-existent for me previously. Putting an end to miscommunication was (and still is, on occasion) challenging.

Honestly, most conversations I have with other people aren't generally mindful. Mindful communication implies being considerate and mindful of our words—it's rarely what we do, as our egos most of the time get involved.

Mindful communication implies shedding consideration and mindfulness on our words. Honestly, most of the conversations I have with other people are rarely mindful. Mindful communication requires us being considerate of others' feelings and mindful of our words.

So instead of speaking thoughtlessly, take time to think a little and keep the other person's feelings in mind.

My relationship with other people prospered when I taught myself the craft of mindful communication. I consistently observed what pestered others and me during my conversations with them. I then tried to discover what connects us with people versus what pushes us away.

How I Learned to Communicate Successfully

Listen. When I was younger, I had the habit of interrupting people as they talked just so that I could talk too. As I grew up, I came to see how much people pull away during discussions when we don't really hear them out.

Listening is the initial move toward mindful communication. Show the other individual that you are a good listener by letting them finish first what they are saying before responding. Likewise, you have to keep your mind concentrated on the speaker rather than letting your thoughts wander somewhere else. Listen intently. Properly tuning into each person's word is an important part of effective communication.

Practice non-judgment. I was a mediator a couple of times throughout my life. Having been one, I picked up a very important lesson. There are always different sides to the story, and none of them is essentially right or off base. Individuals who are fighting or in disagreement will, in general, judge each other during communication. Even when we are on great terms with others, we unknowingly judge them when we don't see their side of the story.

To mindfully talk and evade clashes with other people, we have to try our best to avoid judging other people's opinion, story, or point of view. We should accept the fact that there is no wrong or right—just various perspectives.

Show understanding. A psychologist from Nepal once explained the significance of showing other people that we get them or understand them. He explained how he utilizes this system with his patients. When they reveal to him their issues, the main thing he says is "I get it" or "I understand." It gives them a feeling of solace that their words and sentiments are relatable.

At the day's end, we simply need to feel like we are understood. Applying the non-judgment strategy above enables us to see the bigger picture, and in doing so, it causes us to comprehend their point of view.

Place yourself in their shoes. I've heard a great deal of "You're not in my shoes" or "Place yourself in my shoes." To be "in another person's shoes" is to regard their experience by imagining it's us rather than them.

When we do this, we get to know better what they're feeling. We don't need to wait for them to ask us whether we're getting what they're stating. What I do is that I imagine myself being in that person's shoes, which helps me—again—to develop understanding. Place yourself in somebody else's shoes. Imagining that you are in your confider's position allows you to have the option to understand and express sympathy.

Be absolutely there. It troubles me the most whenever I'm speaking with somebody who is not completely "there" with me. Since I know how upsetting this is, I've tried my best to be completely present in my conversations with others.

Not being available during communication can run from checking your cell phones all the time, sitting in front of the TV, or taking part in whatever else during the communication. To have a fruitful communication, we should set other things aside and thoroughly be with the individual who's talking.

The primary reaction shouldn't be advice or berating. This used to be one of my most prominent issues in the past. I've come to see that many of us do it unknowingly. When it's our turn to respond, our answer is generally something personal.

We either recount a personal story or explain how we personally feel about it. While it's noteworthy to back up our response with our own personal stories and outlook, it's better not to express them at first.

I learned it the hard way that the speaker must be the priority. "I understand," as previously mentioned, can be a decent place to begin. At that point, we can ask the individual how they feel about it and what they will do. We can also ask them to explain their thoughts.

Let go of results. When I was younger, I was always focused on winning, particularly when it came to dialogues. No matter what, I was resolved to be the one winning the talk. I anticipated a result. I wanted other people to agree with me all the time. I only stopped this habit when I understood that waiting for a winning result in every conversation negatively ends the communication.

We should be careful with our words when engaged in a conversation if we want to mindful of other people. Do not take things personally, and always respond in a non-aggressive manner—these are the first steps toward having a mindful conversation.

Try not to hurt others. Buddhism promotes having peaceful conversations with people and avoiding being hash. The thing I like most about Buddhism is the means by which they insist on staying kind and caring with other people during communication. It is important not to hurt others when we are conversing with them. Buddhism states that each destructive word that leaves our mouths is a double-edged sword; it will hurt us as much as it will hurt others.

Chapter 11: Habits of Highly Mindful People

The intention to live a more mindful life is continuing to grow, and more and more people want to follow such a lifestyle. May these tips I share in this chapter help you develop mindfulness. I have the opportunity of knowing some brilliant individuals who are genuinely an inspiration in the manner that they live and breathe mindfulness in their everyday lives.

Some of them have picked to follow the way of life of a priest or swami; however, many of them are regular individuals living regular lives like us. These people all have certain things I've seen that they do differently than most of us, though—things that help them lead a more mindful and satisfying life. Here are the seven key habits of mindful individuals. I have also included some tips on how you can apply these habits into your life.

They Hold Thoughts Lightly

Mindful individuals always observe what's happening in their minds. They focus on the thoughts that are in your mind, yet they hold them lightly. They don't believe their thoughts, and they don't pay attention to them all that. They're likewise eager to scrutinize any adapted examples of thought and conviction that don't serve them.

Through this sort of self-perception, they can step back and watch the mind as opposed to being swept in its current. In this way, they free themselves from molded reactive methods for living and thinking.

Whenever you watch your thoughts, you are being mindful. Begin tuning in to the voice in your mind as regularly as possible, particularly any repetitive thought patterns.

As you listen, be a fair observer. Before long, you'll realize, "There is the voice, and here I am tuning in to it. I am not the mind."

They Feel What They're Feeling

Mindfulness isn't tied in with being always happy. It's about the total acknowledgment of the present moment for what it's worth. That implies feeling what is here to be felt at this time without trying to oppose or control it. Indeed, even highly mindful individuals feel emotional sometimes. They feel outraged, pity, and dread here and there; however, what separates them apart is that they don't try to deny these feelings.

They recognize what they're feeling and allow themselves to feel them as it is. They know that their feelings, both wonderful and upsetting, come and go as part of their life.

That doesn't mean they can't respond to create change. Truth be told, they're able to do so.

They approach problems in life in a mindful manner. A highly mindful person can stay focused and quiet despite everything. They're able to respond instead of reacting, and they make wise decisions.

They realize that what makes us feel satisfied, what brings us the most harmony, is being present in the moment and accepting everything about life—the good and the bad.

They Accept the Transient Nature of Things

Maybe the most fundamental law of life is that everything is always changing. Nothing lasts forever. We can listen with our ears and hear the sounds around us as they, arise, unfurl, and then vanish. We see with our eyes how the seasons change, how things age, and how the world transforms around you.

Sensations, feelings, and musings come and go every which way. We're conceived on this planet, grow, become more seasoned, and in the long run, pass away. Mindful individuals comprehend, acknowledge, and mull over the transient nature of things. Along these lines, they are aware of the value of life, and they enjoy each moment and every day.

Since they acknowledge what is transient, they become immovably established in the quiet perpetual mindfulness that is at the center of their being, the space wherein all that is transient travels every which way.

They Meditate

You can be mindful without contemplating, yet all highly mindful individuals I know have a normal routine with regard to reflection and meditation. Mindful people remain wakeful and present amid the good and bad times of everyday life.

Set aside at least ten minutes per day to meditate, ideally before doing anything else. That way, you will carry with you the energy of mindfulness in the remainder of your day.

They Do One Thing at a Time

There is a myth that performing multiple tasks at once makes us more productive. But the truth is that it drains our energy quicker and makes us less effective. Studies have shown that when people multitask (which is doing several tasks at once), it takes them 50 percent longer to complete a task and they're 50 percent bound to make mistakes.

Mindful people focus only on doing one thing at a time. Mindful people do one assignment at a time with full mindfulness. They do their tasks one by one. They additionally take breaks before proceeding to another assignment. It's a more productive, increasingly effective, and all the more sustainable approach to work and life. Why not try this highly mindful method when studying for the exams in the following week? See how it feels.

They Turn Everyday Tasks into Mindful Moments

Quite a bit of our day-by-day life is taken up by regular tasks—for example, housework, shopping, driving, dressing, and showering. Rather than considering routine exercises as "simply exhausting tasks," profoundly mindful individuals use their time doing these tasks to be mindful.

For example, when folding clothes, they don't essentially race through it to complete it immediately. Rather, they relish the experience, feeling the texture of the surfaces and maybe seeing how crisp they smell. Indeed, even doing the laundry turns into a kind of meditation to work on, moving carefully, mindful to each fold. Thus, each and every action turns into a sacred custom.

Maybe you could pick one task (brushing your teeth, for instance) and try making it your mindful practice. Doing this, you may before long come to understand that there is no such thing as a dull moment, just dull perspectives.

They Nurture and Protect their Mind and Body

Mindful individuals are overseers of their bodies and minds. They make a habit of tuning in to their bodies and minds and observing what is nourishing and what is depleting. They purposely and effectively develop healthy ways of being.

They additionally maintain unhealthy methods of being. They give cautious consideration to what they consume. They make sure that they eat well and get enough rest and exercise.

They're also mindful so as not to feed their minds with "lousy nourishment," such as long hours of watching TV, excessive internet surfing, thoughtless gaming, violence, and useless magazines.

It doesn't mean that mindful people never enjoy a glass of wine or watch movies. It just implies that they mostly have nourishing things in their lives and not too much that is depleting.

They treat their minds and bodies with adoration and regard, realizing that being caring to themselves is a way of showing affection toward all life and makes mindful living a lot simpler.

Practical Strategies for Better Communication in the Relationship

When you look at a couple, can you instantly say if

they have a good relationship or not? It is impossible to completely know what goes on behind the curtain, to be honest. However, when you look at two people together and observe them for a little while, you can usually tell a lot about their relationship. The way they talk to each other, their body language, and their overall manner will tell you how happy or unfortunately unhappy they are together.

For instance, you might see two people sitting at a table in a restaurant. They sit across each other and are making agitated gestures as they talk. This shows they are unhappy at the time and fighting. You can tell this even when you can't hear what they are talking about. There might by another couple that is sitting at another table. These two sit right beside each other and are looking at each other happily as they talk. They might even be arguing over something, but they don't look unhappy about it. This is because the second couple has a better understanding of each other. They respect their opinions even when they argue. This allows them to be present and enjoy their moments together despite it all. But you shouldn't assume that a good relationship happens overnight. Two people don't just meet and live happily ever after together forever.

A good relationship requires real commitment, effort, compromise, and effective communication. It is easy for two people to fall in love. The tough part comes later when they have to stay with each other and keep the romance alive even when they discover just how different they are. Even when there is love, there can be conflict. You have to understand that each person can have a different way of loving. This is why one might not be able to understand or be receptive of the other's love. This is where proper communication comes in. You both have to learn how to navigate through conflict and express love in the way that your partner needs it. It is not enough just to show love as you want to. You need to consider the other person's wants and needs. Communication is required so that you can let each other know what your expectations are.

By now, you have a much better understanding of how you need to be more mindful and communicate better with your partner. If you fail to communicate with your partner, you will never be able to understand them and support them in the way they need. Think of how you feel when they fail to understand you or take your side when you need them. Think of when you make mistakes and they lash out at you. When you place yourself in the other person's shoes, you will be able to have a much clearer perspective in any situation. This will help you avoid unnecessary fights and quarrels with the person you love. A relationship can be a lot of work, but if you put in that effort, it will be for your benefit in the long run.

Since you comprehend communication as a whole now and think differently, how about we plunge into the demonstrated communication techniques we use to impart adequately?

We have used these communication techniques a few times to improve communication in our marriage effectively. They were basic to us, enduring our first year of marriage!

Truly, we firmly trust these communication techniques will fortify communication in your marriage as well. Think about them as tips on the best way to improve communication in marriage.

1. ***Ensure your life partner is tuning in to you and focusing.*** Before you speak with your partner, make sure that their complete attention is focused on you. There is no point in having half their attention while they are mentally somewhere else. Because if your partner isn't tuning in or focusing, every one of your "words" won't be heard. A meaningless conversation like that would just be a waste of time and energy.

2. ***Try not to shout out at your companion.*** It just does not set the tone for better marriage communication. It could put your partner on edge, as well as exasperate them. It may also make them more likely to be non-responsive to

whatever you have to say.

3. *Attempt to see the issue from your partner's perspective.* How might they best comprehend what you are trying to convey to them? Think of them and how they might perceive what you say or do. This will allow you to avoid a misunderstanding before it could even arise. Think of the best way in which you can establish mutual understanding.

4. *Take time to think about what you are attempting to convey.* Try out diverse verbal clarifications. You could likewise utilize the illustration of graphs, letters, and so forth. On the off chance that you realize they like hard information and numbers, or visuals, have a go at utilizing those as it makes communication a ton simpler. Find the best way in which you can put your point across to your partner. If you want to convince them of something, hard facts will do the job. If they're more emotional, use that card.

5. ***Inquire as to whether they understand what you are trying to tell them.*** Give them a chance to repeat it to you if they comprehend you. Keep checking in to see if they understand whatever you just told them. You can clarify any doubts they have along the way. By clearing up, you will take out any presumptions that might lead to misunderstandings.

6. ***On the off chance that the above does not work or you start to feel a little confused, enjoy a reprieve.*** Return to it later after each of you has had some time and space to consider the issue properly. Taking a break will likewise help in clearing your mind and thoughts.

Practice the six techniques above for the following seven days. You will see incredible improvement by the way you speak with your companion from here on forward. Your relationship will likewise show signs of improvement. You need to use all that you have learned in this book to help you improve your relationship for the better. Think before you speak or react. Take time to process emotions and thoughts and allow the same for your partner. Show them that you love and care and respect them. Be more open and welcoming and let them know that you want better communication in your relationship. Things will improve for the better.

Chapter 12: The Power of Gratitude

What Is Gratitude?

Gratitude is being thankful and acknowledging or appreciating whatever is good in your life or any kindness someone else shows you. You may not realize it, but gratitude has immense power. It can potentially change your life for the better. An act of gratitude can help you apologize, solve conflicts, and make amends in your relationship. Being grateful will be intrinsically rewarding for you in the long run.

When you realize that all that you have is not guaranteed for tomorrow, your sense of gratitude will automatically be stronger. So stop taking your partner and your happy relationship for granted. Show them that you are grateful for having them in your life and for all that they do for you. If you are happy in your relationship, you can use the power of gratitude to manifest more positivity in your relationship and your life. The law of attraction will pull more good into your relationship when you show that you appreciate what you already have.

Benefits of Gratitude

- Improvement in physical, mental, and spiritual well-being
- Improvement in social relationships
- Greater feelings and thoughts of happiness and increased optimism
- Increased connection with others in times of loss or any crisis
- Higher levels of energy
- Improved emotional intelligence
- Decreased blood pressure
- Healthier cardiovascular system
- Higher capacity to forgive others
- Decreased level of stress, anxiety, or depression
- Improvement in efforts for self-care
- Increased sense of spirituality
- Higher likelihood to lead a healthier lifestyle

Impact of Gratitude in Your Relationship

In terms of marriage or relationship, gratitude plays

an important role in it as well. Gratefulness will help you take notice of all that is good in your relationship. A lot of people tend to stop looking at the good in their partner and start focusing on the bad at some point. It's great fun at the beginning of the relationship, but things tend to go south from there. You will be more inclined to notice what your partner doesn't do for you or lacks instead of focusing on all that they do and have done for you. People fail to notice that giving and taking has to be both ways. Your partner might make less of an effort in your relationship if you don't make much either.

Expectations increase, but actions take a back seat. Everyone is waiting for the other to do more and prove their worth. But what if you retrain your mind and start over. Why don't you start paying attention to the little things that your partner has always been doing for you? These little things are often more significant than the grand gestures you are waiting for. They might not bring you flowers as often anymore, but they still make sure to do the dishes at night for you. Your partner might not get all dressed up every time you go out now, but they always make sure your laundry is done. Things would be so much better in your relationship if you started thinking about the good instead of the bad. And it's not just about thinking. It is important to express gratitude. You need to let the other person know that you appreciate all that they do for you. Appreciation gives validation to their efforts.

When you stop thanking them or showing some form of appreciation, they will lack the will to do much for you. Gratitude will do so much for you personally and for your relationship. It will instill happiness and positivity in your partner. They will appreciate the fact that you take time to express your appreciation of their actions as well. You have to create this kind of positive cycle in your relationship, not one where both keep blaming each other for what the other doesn't do or how little they care. All the complaining and cribbing will only make things go downhill in your relationship. But using words and actions to show that you are grateful will make a lot of difference.

Gratefulness needs to be cultivated in your mind so that it becomes the natural way you always think. It will help you see what is going right in your life even when other things may go wrong. The law of attraction allows better things to come your way when you focus on what is good. If you stop taking note of the good things and focus on the bad things, you will attract more negativity. Expressing gratitude to the universe for all that you have will push more blessings your way. So start cultivating this habit of gratitude. Show that you appreciate a good weather day, a day off, a good meal, a fun date with your partner, or anything that makes you smile or makes your life easier. No matter how hard your life may seem at times, remember that some people have it much tougher. The small things you take for granted are often what others have been striving for their entire lives. You will be able to achieve your dreams and goals at some point if you stop worrying and doubting. Think of the good that has happened, and thank the universe for it. Believe that you will be blessed with more.

Ways to Cultivate Gratitude

The following tips will help you cultivate gratitude every single day in your life.

Keep a gratitude journal. One of the easiest ways to cultivate a sense of gratitude is to keep a gratitude journal. I have personally been doing this for years, and I know it helps immensely. Adding this one positive exercise to your everyday routine will barely take any time, but the benefit will increase in multiples over time. This gratitude journal will allow you to keep a record for all the things and experiences you are grateful for in your life.

Try to take a few minutes and write down at least three positive things from a particular day. You can appreciate and be grateful for the bigger blessings in your life, but this journaling will allow you to take notice of the smaller ones as well. For instance, you can be grateful for a day with cool winds during a hot summer. You can be grateful for the nice meal you had or even something like a good conversation you shared with a friend. When you record such positive things down, it will help you create a habit of thinking positively. You will be more alert and appreciative of all the good things that happen every day.

Most people these days choose to notice only what goes wrong in their day and focus on that. This cultivates negativity. You can counter this behavior and cultivate gratitude and positivity in your life. The gratitude journal will help you be more enthusiastic about your days and more determined to make the next day a good one as well.

You might face challenges, and something bad might happen on some days. But you can choose to focus on the things that went right instead. Many studies have been conducted on the impact of gratitude journaling, and they have all shown positive results.

People who practice gratitude journaling tend to be happier and more positive.

Focus on gratitude for a few minutes at the end of every day. Take some deep breaths and think of the things you are grateful for. Thank the higher powers for your blessings and your ability to overcome any challenges that come your way. Be mindful and present as you do this gratitude exercise. Think of all the good things that happened to you throughout your day. If some person helped in making your day better, write a thank-you note to them and pass it on the next day.

Let your partner know that they are appreciated. Tell them that you are thankful that they helped in making your day good and that they made you happy. Expressing gratitude to them will make them appreciate this gesture and feel appreciated too. If your partner made you a good meal or just took time to ask about your day, thank them for it. Show them that you are grateful for their efforts and their presence in your life.

Avoid complaining as much as possible. When you constantly crib or complain about something, you are focused on the negativity of the day. Instead, choose to let it go. If you can improve something, spend your energy on working on it instead of complaining. If you have no control over it, avoid obsessing over it.

Every morning when you wake up, take some time to express gratitude. Think of the things you are grateful for and what you hope for the day as well. Repeat some positive affirmations and watch them unfold into reality.

Gratitude meditation is another way to build positivity. It is a way to train your mind to be more positive, grateful, and happy. Spending a few minutes meditating every day will benefit you a lot in the long term. Find a comfortable place to be seated and relax. Close your mind and take a few abdominal breaths slowly and steadily. Try to feel more grounded where you are seated. When you feel more relaxed, ask yourself what you are grateful for. Think about any one of those things and ponder on it. Absorb the positivity from that grateful incident or thought. Continue to another experience you are grateful for. Try to visualize all this happening once again in your mind. This is how you create a positive chain of thought in your mind. It is important to continually remind yourself of your positive experiences because humans tend to hold on to negative experiences more often. Break that chain and let go of the negativity instead.

Being grateful can transform your life in so many different ways, and all of them are positive. Your focus will shift from what you lack to everything that you have and should be grateful for. Gratitude will give you the power to see all the possibilities and opportunities that lie ahead of you in life and to look forward to them all. Be grateful for the blessings and learn to anticipate more instead of dreading something negative from happening.

Conclusion

As we come to the end of this book, I would like to thank you for investing your time and effort in reading through it. I hope it was a good read and that it helped you understand the communication issues that you might have been facing trouble with. By now, you should have a better perspective on the important role of communication in a healthy relationship.

When you blame, fail to listen, or choose to say hurtful things to your partner, you cause pain not only for them but also for yourself. A little bit of understanding and effort can go a long way in fixing even the biggest of issues. You have to understand that your relationship should be a source of strength and happiness for both you and your partner. You should both be able to freely express yourself and be assured of validation when you need it. It's not about agreeing on all things even when you disagree. Instead, it's about picking your fights and expressing yourself in the right way.

The right words, tone of voice, and body language will play a big role in your relationship. Try using the suggestions that are given in this book, and you will see the small bit significant difference they make. You will make mistakes along the way, but the fact that you are reading this book shows that you are making an effort in the right direction. Slowly but surely, you will see the miracles that good communication can result in for your relationship.

References

Are you expressing your anger constructively or destructively? (2019). Retrieved from https://www1.cbn.com/biblestudy/are-you-expressing-your-anger-constructively-or-destructively%3F

Boissiere, E. (2019). 5 misunderstandings that will cause problems in your closest relationships. Retrieved from https://everydaypowerblog.com/reasons-for-a-misunderstanding-in-relationships/

Communication skills that can strengthen any relationship. (2019). Retrieved from https://www.verywellmind.com/managing-conflict-in-relationships-communication-tips-3144967

Communication skills: definitions and Examples. (2019). Retrieved from https://www.indeed.co.in/career-advice/resumes-cover-letters/communication-skills

Constructive anger: using rage to your advantage. (2019). Retrieved from https://www.verywellmind.com/constructive-anger-2797286

5 signs ego is ruining your relationship. (2019). Retrieved from https://www.powerofpositivity.com/5-signs-ego-is-ruining-your-relationship/amp/

How can we communicate better? (2019). Retrieved from https://www.loveisrespect.org/healthy-relationships/communicate-better/

How can we communicate better? (2019). Retrieved from https://www.loveisrespect.org/healthy-relationships/communicate-better

How couples misunderstand each other (2019). Retrieved from https://www.psychologytoday.com/intl/blog/a

nger-in-the-age-entitlement/201607/how-couples-misunderstand-each-other?amp

How ego kills the relationships. (2019). Retrieved from https://medium.com/@ns.nimra.shehzadi/how-ego-kills-the-relationships-a34a965812f2

How to avoid misunderstandings in relationships (2019). Retrieved from https://www.aha-now.com/how-to-avoid-misunderstanding-others/amp/

Keys to effective communication in marriage. (2019). Retrieved from https://firstthings.org/keys-to-effective-communication-in-marriage

Ohlin, B. (2019). 7 ways to improve communication in relationships [Update 2019]. Retrieved from https://positivepsychologyprogram.com/communication-in-relationships/

The 15 most common relationship problems and how to fix each one of them. (2019). Retrieved from https://thoughtcatalog.com/ioana-casapu/2017/04/the-15-most-common-relationship-problems-and-how-to-fix-each-one-of-them/

The battle of ego vs. love. (2019). Retrieved from https://psiloveyou.xyz/the-fight-of-ego-vs-love-70cd450a4742

The healing power of gratitude (2019). Retrieved from https://www.psychologytoday.com/intl/blog/compassion-matters/201511/the-healing-power-gratitude?amp

The key to communication in relationships (2019). Retrieved from https://www.tonyrobbins.com/ultimate-relationship-guide/key-communication-relationships/

The power of gratitude. (2019). Retrieved from https://www.successconsciousness.com/guest_articles/power_of_gratitude.htm

The transformative power of gratitude. (2019).
Retrieved from
https://www.huffpost.com/entry/the-transformative-power_n_6982152

Therapist, F., Us, W., & Us, C. (2019). 10 effective
communication skills in relationships.
Retrieved from
https://www.marriage.com/advice/relationship/effective-relationship-communication-skills/amp/

Understanding validation: a way to communicate
acceptance (2019). Retrieved from
https://www.psychologytoday.com/us/blog/pieces-mind/201204/understanding-validation-way-communicate-acceptance?amp

Validation: the most powerful relationship skill you
were never taught. (2019). Retrieved from
https://michaelssorensen.com/2017/12/20/validation-the-most-powerful-relationship-skill-you-were-never-taught/

Made in the USA
Monee, IL
18 December 2019